CIRCUS PARADE

Frontispiece

1 'MISS LOLA AT THE CIRQUE FERNANDO'
*From the Painting by Degas
in The Tate Gallery, London*

CIRCUS PARADE

By
JOHN S. CLARKE

★

*Illustrated from
Old Prints and Pictures, and
Modern Photographs*

This edition digitally re-mastered and
published by JM Classic Editions © 2008
Original text © John S Clarke 1936

ISBN 978-1-905217-92-2

All rights reserved. No part of this book subject
to copyright may be reproduced in any form or
by any means without prior permission in writing
from the publisher.

FOREWORD

THIS is a book of circus lore. It has been written for entertainment—and instruction. It is not a history, though it contains much that is historical.

When watching some spectacular act in the ring, some breathless feat of daring and endurance or, maybe, an equine ballet of subtle charm, I have often felt sorry for performers and spectators alike. For the performers because they did not receive the appreciation they deserved; for the spectators because they did not rightly understand what was taking place. They were entertained and they applauded, but had they known more about it both their delight and their response would have been enhanced.

I have set myself the task of interpreting the circus to the uninitiated. I do hope I have succeeded.

My own connection with the circus world covers a period of thirty-five years. I was a rough-rider when only ten years of age; a performer with wild animals at sixteen, and a trainer of horses and wild beasts at twenty-two. Some of my experiences are embodied in the following chapters. To those who object that I have intruded myself too scantily I can only reply that this is a book on circus life, not an autobiography. The theme is greater than the individual.

Once a circus man, always a circus man. It is twenty-six years ago that Fate decided that my connection with the circus in any professional capacity should cease. I accepted a post offered to me by Edward Bostock of Glasgow, and then rejected it for one in Edinburgh as a lecturer and writer. That was in the year 1910. Twenty-two years later, after a varied life in journalism and politics, I was privileged to wind up the career of the oldest travelling show on earth—Bostock and Wombwell's Menagerie—by delivering the valedictory speech to the staff in the Kelvin Hall, Glasgow.

Not once during all those years was I able to keep away from the circus. The odour of tan and sawdust, and of the stables and animal dens, never left my nostrils. The glitter of arc-lamps (and naphtha flares), of paint, fleshings, spangles and sequins, was ever in my eyes. Circus gets in the blood and cannot be eradicated.

There are one or two things not dealt with in the book which ought to be mentioned here. Has the circus a jargon of its own? It has not. Circus folk very seldom talk the slang of the showground. The circus has a vocabulary like every other profession or art, but it is not a slang vocabulary. The expression 'Big Top,' meaning the great tent, is a fairly recent importation from America. There they also speak of the 'White Top.' If a circus artiste speaks slang at all it is the current slang of the day.

It is a fairly common belief, too, that the circus folk are largely Romany. This is a mistake. One seldom sees a gipsy in the circus, and there is still an element of distrust among circus folk for the gipsies. Gipsies will be found on every showground, but they have their own methods of earning a livelihood, and circus work is certainly not one of them.

I have written little of the private life of the circus people because it no more concerns the reader than does my own private life. They eat, drink, love, marry, beget children, and not infrequently curse and swear like everyday citizens. Their art may be the public's, but their domestic concerns are their own. That these are as wholesome and regular as those of any section of the stabilised community I can assure the reader.

One word about the illustrations. Not one of them is faked in any way, not even 'retouched.' Those depicting the acts are from photographs taken during the actual performance. Never before has such a wonderful series of circus pictures been presented to the public. I am immensely proud of the fact that this circus epic has been issued by the firm of Batsford —makers of beautiful books.

JOHN S. CLARKE

GLASGOW,
   November 1936

ACKNOWLEDGMENT

The Publishers must acknowledge their obligation to the photographers whose work is reproduced in these pages, namely, the Alfieri Picture Service, for Fig. 65; Associated Scottish Newspapers, for Fig. 15; Mr. Charles E. Brown, for Figs. 12, 29, 30, 34, 38, 39, 40, 43, 54, 60, 62, 64, 68, 70, 72, 73, 80, 83, 97, 126, 127, 128, 139; the Central Press, for Figs. 13, 69; Mr. William Davis (the General Photographic Agency) for Figs. 10, 32, 47, 48, 55, 74, 76, 79, 87, 88, 94, 95, 98, 123, 131; the *Daily Mail*, for Fig. 51; Fox Photos, for Figs. 21, 33, 75, 90; the Keystone View Co., for Figs. 18, 22, 49, 50, 61, 106, 122, 133, 135; Mr. Bob Leavith, for Figs. 20, 59, 136, 137; Schrammen, for Figs. 27, 28; W. Seldow, for Figs. 81, 82, 86; Sport and General, for Figs. 45, 46, 53, 89, 91, 130, 132; *The Times*, for Figs. 52, 129; the Topical Press Agency, for Figs. 44, 84; Hedda Walther, for Fig. 107; Wide World Photos, for Figs. 3, 25, 56, 58, 63, 71, 125, 138. The front and back endpapers are reproduced from photographs by the *Daily Express* and Mr. Charles E. Brown respectively. Fig. 5 is included by courtesy of the Proprietors of *The Sphere*, and of the Artist, Mr. F. Matania.

Special thanks are due to Mr. Bertram Mills, who very kindly placed his extensive photographic library at the publishers' disposal, and to Herr Robert Wilschke for his help in the collection of the photographs. Most of the remaining illustrations, including those from historic sources, are from the Author's collection.

CONTENTS

		PAGE
	FOREWORD	v
	ACKNOWLEDGMENT	vii
I.	CIRCUS ORIGINS	1
II.	SAWDUST AND SPANGLE-LAND	19
III.	CIRCUS HORSES	27
IV.	UP IN THE DOME	38
V.	THE CIRCUS SPIRIT	45
VI.	CLOWNS AND CLOWNING	54
VII.	ACROBATS, JUGGLERS AND WIRE-DANCERS	64
VIII.	MAN AND BEAST	71
IX.	'LION TAMERS' OF OLD	80
X.	THE MODERNS	91
XI.	THE CIRCUS IN AMERICA	105
XII.	CONCLUSION	115
	INDEX	117

2 The Author and Simba

3 The Medrano Sisters: one of the most graceful acts of to-day

I

CIRCUS ORIGINS

ROMAN gladiators fought their duels in the circus long before an even more degenerate age transferred such spectacles to the amphitheatre. Before their entry they paused before the royal box, gave the fascist salute, and cried to Cæsar, 'Those about to die salute thee!'

An obliging and courteous body of men were the gladiators. They had to be, for they were of the slave class. They fought each other with cunning weapons like net and trident, or in straightforward manner with *gladius* or *cesti* (knuckledusters). One group, for they were strictly specialised, were called *Bestiarii*, their combats being with wild beasts instead of men. This form of entertainment originated with the establishment of the *Venationes*, or wild beast games, under M. Fulvius Nobilor, in 186 B.C.

The exhibition of strange animals from foreign lands where Roman arms triumphed was not enough for the bloodthirsty Roman mob. Accordingly lion fought lion in the circus of 95 B.C., but the following year, under Sulla, 100 lions were shot down in public by a picked body of Moorish dartmen.[1] From this time onward the spectacle of animal torture and butchery grew in popularity until the number of creatures destroyed transcends belief. Pompeius during his second consulship (55 B.C.) caused 500 lions, 18 elephants, and 410 leopards to be killed in five days. Julius Cæsar went one better by turning 400 lions loose at once—to be destroyed by archers and javelin throwers. Livy caps all this by telling, in Book XXXIX, 22, how Trojan, on his return from Dacia, butchered 11,000 animals to make a record holiday.

At times business of state was combined with popular pleasure. The more ferocious exhibits were made public executioners. Thus, long before Christians were thrown to the lions, deserters at the Punic war were similarly despatched

[1] Valerius Maximus, Book XI, vii.

by Scipio during his Triumph (146 B.C.). He had, however, merely copied a predecessor, Lucius Æmilius Paullus, who had his deserters in the war against Perseus trampled to death by elephants in the Circus Flaminius (168 B.C.).[1]

To the religion of the Greeks and Romans we must attribute much that is revolting in their practices. Both people firmly believed that the spirits of the dead took delight at the shedding of blood. To this belief may be traced the custom of slaughtering captives at the funeral pyres of ancient warriors, as well as the spectacles already mentioned, which incarnadine the pages of Roman history for over five centuries. When such were transferred to 'more convenient premises,' namely the amphitheatres like the Colosseum, the circus returned to its legitimate performance.

An amphitheatre (the word means *theatre all round*) differed from a theatre in much the same way as a modern circus at Olympia differs from a typical theatre of to-day. Raised seats, tier after tier, encircled the arena, which was sunk below ground-level in order that the spectators in the lowest row of seats might not be exposed to danger from the wild beasts. Doors from the arena led to passages communicating with apartments used by various combatants and with the dens which housed the wild animals. There was no roof, but at the Colosseum a *vela* or awning was spread overhead on scorching hot days. The stone sockets which supported the poles of the awning are still visible on the outer wall of the building.

The circus was entirely different, both structurally and in its form of entertainment. Neither institution, by the way, had the remotest connection with the circus of to-day, but it is necessary to make this clear.

The Roman circus was an oblong building, semicircular at one end. A description of one, the Circus Maximus, will serve for all, for they varied little and then only in non-essentials. The most complete description of the great building erected by Tarquinius and destined to become one of the most beautiful adornments of the city will be found in Dionysius (III, 68). It was three stadia and a half long (700 yards) four plethra; in breadth (135 yards); and could seat 150,000 persons. Altered

[1] Valerius Maximus, Book XI, vii.

4 The Amphitheatre at Pompeii

5 The Roman Circus: a Reconstruction by F. Matania

and extended by various emperors, it is said to have accommodated over 400,000 spectators in the fourth century, but this is too difficult to swallow. The seats were supported by a triple row of porticoes, one above the other. The vast arena was divided by a *spina*, a raised structure like a wall, but adorned with monuments, columns, pinnacles and statues. At the straight end of the arena were the arched *carceres*—starting-places for the racing chariots, which were closed towards the arena but could be opened simultaneously to allow the chariots to dash out. Just below the *metae* (pinnacles) at the end of the *spina*, a chalk-line (*alba linea*) was drawn across the sanded floor of the arena. This was the 'winning-post.' Certain religious ceremonies opened the circus shows (*Ludi Circenses*) which consisted of military spectacles, athletic sports, but chiefly of chariot and horse-racing contests. Chariots were drawn by four horses (*Quadrigae*) by two horses (*Bigae*) or by three (*Trigae*).

From four to six chariots dashed from the unbarred *carceres*, made the circuit of the *spina* seven times and drove off the course through the barriers on the left side of the *spina*. Seven circuits constituted one heat or *missus*, and the number of these varied from ten to twenty-four. The charioteer stood in his chariot, dressed in a sleeveless tunic belted around the body and wearing a helmet-shaped cap. He held a whip in his hand and carried a knife in his girdle to cut the reins with, if any accident happened, for these were attached to his girdle. Chariots and tunics were decked with the colours of the *factions*—white, red, green, blue, purple and gold being the best known. During the race, mounted 'seconds' accompanied the chariots to cheer on the driver. At times these men raced each other as *desultores*, each man having two horses and vaulting from one to the other as they galloped down the arena.

In equestrian displays of this kind, and in some of the athletic sports (which included prize-fighting), the Roman Circus approached the performance of to-day—but not very closely. Nothing fundamental links the two together in any kind of relationship.

The Roman Circus with its games, *Ludi Circenses*, is the ancestor of the modern race-course, racing track, and 'stadium';

the amphitheatre that of the bull-ring, bear-garden, and in some measure of the prize-ring, but in neither of them can we trace the origins of the modern circus.

II

MUSICIAN AND DANCING HORSE
After a fourteenth-century illuminated MS.

After Rome, barbarism, the 'Dark Ages' and Medievalism. One thinks of the glee-men, the minstrels—trouveres or troubadours—the mountebank and jongleurs, 'saunterers' all, without home or even land (*sans terre*).

In Anglo-Saxon days they wandered from camp to camp, from court to court, sometimes in strange company. In the illuminated manuscripts one may see miniatures depicting, graphically enough, wayside entertainers of those far far-off times. Charles Knight, of *Old England* fame, reproduced many of these in wood-cut. We see solitary musicians playing to dancing men and dancing bears, horses beating the tabor with their forefeet, and little monkeys turning somersaults while a thrilled audience applauds. In the thirteenth and fourteenth centuries jugglers are in evidence, and tumblers are doing elegant flip-flaps on the village green. In the seventh volume of *Archeologia* there is an account of a 'rope-flying' performance in the reign of Edward VI. Strutt, in his *Sports*, quotes from it:

MOUNTEBANK AND DANCING DOG
After a medieval MS.

'There was a great rope, as great as the cable of a ship, stretched from the battlements of Paul's Steeple, with a great anchor at one end, fastened a little before the Dean of Paul's house-gate and when his Majesty approached near the same, there came a man, a stranger, being a native of Arragon, lying on the rope with his head forward, casting his arms and legs abroad, running on his breast on the rope from the battlements to the ground as if he had been an arrow from a bow, and stayed on the ground.'

THE PERFORMING BEAR
After a fourteenth-century illuminated MS.

In the next reign lived the celebrated Banks, whose educated horse 'Morocco' astonished not only England but France and Italy, and was nearly responsible for Banks being burned to death at Orleans as a sorcerer. Sir Walter Raleigh paid Banks the compliment of saying that had he lived in older times 'he would have shamed all the enchanters in the world; for whosoever was most famous among them could never master or instruct any beast as he did.' Yet the tricks performed by Morocco seem elementary enough to-day. Shakespeare, in *Love's Labour Lost*, Ben Jonson, Sir William Davenant, Pepys and Evelyn, all make allusions to Banks or his marvellous horse. Performing horses were rarities and Banks made money by exhibiting his equine curiosity in the yard of La Belle Sauvage. He was, therefore, a real showman, and his horse a true forerunner of the 'educated' ponies of the circus. From Pepys we gather that Banks set a fashion in entertainment, for at Bartholomew Fair the diarist saw another learned horse.

His entry (1 Sept. 1668) records: 'To Bartholomew Fair, and there saw several sights; among others, the mare that tells money and many things to admiration, and among others come to me, when she was bid to go to him of the company that most loved to kiss a pretty wench in a corner. And this did cost me 12*d.* to the horse, which I had flung him before, and did give

BANKS AND HIS HORSE 'MOROCCO'
From a sixteenth-century woodcut

me occasion to kiss a mighty *belle fille* that was exceeding plain, but *forte belle*.' But educated horses do not make a circus, though it would not be a circus without them.

From very early times it has been the custom to exercise, and begin the breaking, of horses by *lungeing* them. The trainer holds the lungeing-rein while the animal trots in a circle. The circle is known as the lungeing ring, and around an ordinary lungeing ring arose the first of modern circuses. Its founder

6 Astley's: the first Circus Ring

7 Astley's Amphitheatre, Westminster Bridge Road. From an Aquatint in Ackermann's *Microcosm of London*

8 A Liberty Act of Seventy Years Ago

9 Southwark Fair. From an Engraving after Hogarth

was Phillip Astley, a native of Newcastle-under-Lyne, a one-time cavalryman whose feats of equitation had long astonished his military comrades.

Born in 1742 Astley, after serving an apprenticeship to his father, a cabinet-maker, enlisted at seventeen in the 15th regiment of light-horse commanded by General Elliot. Soon his aptitude for riding was brought to the notice of the regimental chiefs, and he became rough-rider and instructor in horsemanship. He served abroad during the last years of the Seven Years War, attained the rank of sergeant-major and obtained his discharge from the army. On leaving the regiment General Elliot presented him with a charger, and upon this horse he gave his first public exhibitions of trick equestrianism in a field near the Halfpenny Hatch, Lambeth. It is perfectly true that men named Price and Samson were giving similar exhibitions at Islington and elsewhere before Astley began. These men, however, did not found the circus. *Astley did.* Removing to a timber-yard in the Westminster Bridge Road, he erected a wooden building, unroofed, with seating accommodation, and here in the year 1780 the first genuine circus performance took place, for combined with the prodigious feats of equitation by Astley, Griffin, Jones and Miller, were acrobatic displays (tumbling); rope-vaulting 'in different attitudes'; a 'knockabout' act with chairs and ladders; an 'Egyptian pyramid' of men, and even a clown, one Burt, who performed as a fill-in and gave an equestrian *entrée*.

Astley's popularity was undoubted, and it was in the nature of things that rivals should arrive. The most formidable one was Hughes, who established the Royal Circus in Blackfriars Road (this afterwards became the Surrey Theatre). Hughes, like Astley, who was six feet in height, was a splendid specimen of manhood and undoubtedly a fine horseman. In an advertisement preserved by Frost there is a covert sneer at Astley, whose success irritated his less fortunate competitors:

'The celebrated Sobieska Clementina and Mr. Hughes on Horseback will end on Monday next, the 4th of October; until then they will display the whole of their performances, which are allowed, by those who know best, to be the completest of the kind in Europe. Hughes humbly thanks the Nobility etc., for the honour of their support, and also acquaints them his Antagonist has catched a bad cold so near to Westminster Bridge, and for his recovery has gone to a warmer climate, which is Bath in Somersetshire. He boasts, poor Fellow, no more of activity, and is now turned Conjurer, in the character of "Sieur the Great." Therefore Hughes is unrivalled, and will perform his surprising feats accordingly at his Horse Academy, until the above day.'

The nose of the patriotic Scot who recollects that Prince Charlie's mother was the Princess Clementina Sobieska of Poland, and that his romantic hero was in exile at the time of this announcement, will possibly curl a little at the astute showman's exploitation of the name. Hughes and his proprietor did not last long. They were burdened with debt, a new partner did not help matters, and, try as they might, they could not even partially eclipse the Astley sun. Hughes was succeeded in management by Grimaldi (an Italian or Portuguese) whose grandson, Joseph, became the greatest clown of the nineteenth century.

The equestrian performances at these earliest of circuses were weird as well as sensational. We read of Mrs. Hughes riding 'at full speed standing on pint pots' and mounting 'pot by pot, higher still, to the terror of all who see her.' At Astley's, the riding troupe, headed by father, mother and son, performed 'upwards of fifty' feats of horsemanship every night and insisted (*vide* programme) on the audience seeing to it that every one was successfully accomplished.

Astley's had many ups and downs during the lifetimes of its founders. Phillip went to prison for running unlicensed entertainments, but was liberated at the request of Lord Thurlow. Father and son went for a time to Paris at the behest of Queen Marie Antoinette, and there, in partnership with Franconi, established the first circus in France. The Queen thought young Astley so handsome that she called him the English Rose.

In 1794 the Westminster Road amphitheatre caught fire and was burned to the ground. It was soon re-erected, but another fire gutted it in 1803. For a time John Astley, the son, in

10 Springboard Acrobats in a Spanish Town

11 The Four Kemmys: a colourful 'Classic' of agility

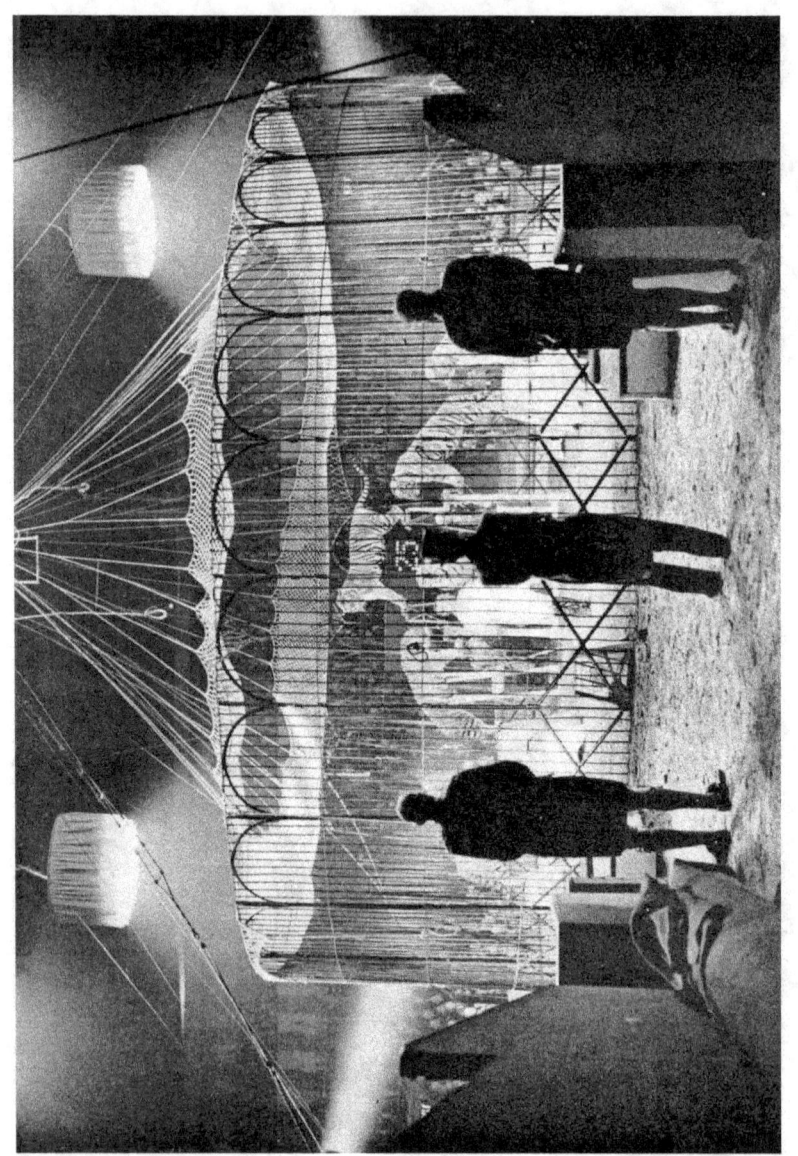

12 The Circus To-day: Trubka and his 'Tiger Pyramid'

partnership with Davis, took over the lease of the third building, which was opened in 1804. The following year a fire completely destroyed the Royal Circus and Astley's had it much their own way. The entertainment was now more varied than ever. Pantomimes, shadowgraphs, musical *entrées* and dancing horses appeared on the programmes. Horace Walpole laments the absence in France of Astley in a letter to Lord Stafford:

> 'London at this time of the year, is as nauseous a drug as any in an apothecary's shop. I could find nothing at all to do and so went to Astley's, which, indeed, was much beyond my expectation. I do not wonder any longer that Darius was chosen king by the instructions he gave to his horse; nor that Caligula made his Consul. Astley can make his dance minuets and hornpipes. But I shall not have even Astley now: Her Majesty the Queen of France, who has as much taste as Caligula, has sent for the whole of the *dramatis personæ* to Paris.'

'Circus' became the fashion in London, to the dismay of the theatre proprietors, who complained bitterly at times at the wholesale desertion of their patrons. The ponderous Dr. Johnson indulged a customary growl at the phenomenon; 'Whitefield,' he said, 'never drew as much attention as a mountebank does. He does not draw attention by doing better than others but by doing what was strange. Were Astley to preach a sermon standing on his head, or on a horse's back, he would collect a multitude to hear him; but no wise man would say he had made a better sermon for that.'

Such then was the origin of the modern circus. To Phillip Astley all the credit, for there can be no doubt that but for his shrewdness and energy, apart altogether from his native talent, the circus performance which consisted solely of equestrian feats would have waned in popularity. In varying the programme by the introduction of novel, bizarre, and spectacular numbers he not only solved the problem of popular appeal (an economic one after all), but he originated an entirely new and ever fascinating form of entertainment. Astley was the greatest horse-trainer of his time. He wrote several treatises on the subject and though lacking any literary distinction, the ideas there advanced were adopted and practised for at least half a century. He died in Paris of gout in the stomach in 1814 and was succeeded by his handsome and clever son John. John's reign, however, was brief. He followed his father to the grave in 1821 dying, strange to relate, 'on the same day of the year, in the same house, and in the same room' as his distinguished parent.

III

Within thirty years of the founding of Astley's 'Amphitheatre and Riding School' the circus became international.

'Astley's' is the most honoured and respected name in circus annals, for the wooden erection at the Lambeth end of Westminster Bridge became the cradle of all circuses. It was Phillip himself who trained the first Batty, Abraham Saunders and Hengler. Now we shall have to tread somewhat warily, for dynasties begin to arise, prodigies appear from nowhere, a matrimonial maze ensues, a new world comes into being. Whoever is foolish enough to attempt to write a history of the circus and of circus families will perish in a madhouse.

A world of bohemianism, nomadism and genius offers enticement to the explorer, but if he looks for records he will be disappointed. They are few, and these are often scrappy, and more frequently contradictory. Out of such fragments we may not be able to weave a complete counterpane but we can, at least, fashion a patchwork quilt and enjoy the fashioning. There were Saunders and Bannister for instance, both associated with Astley's. Miss Bannister, daughter of the above, was Astley's equestrienne the year John Astley died. Her father was one of the earliest circus proprietors to go on tour and the very first to take a circus to Scotland. His scene-painter and part-time mummer was a young house-painter named David Roberts. Roberts left the circus when Bannister became bankrupt, went back to house-painting, was appointed scene-painter to the Pantheon Theatre, Edinburgh, at twenty-five shillings per week, and later earned thirty shillings at the

13 Modern Exotics: a Chinese Acrobat Act at Olympia

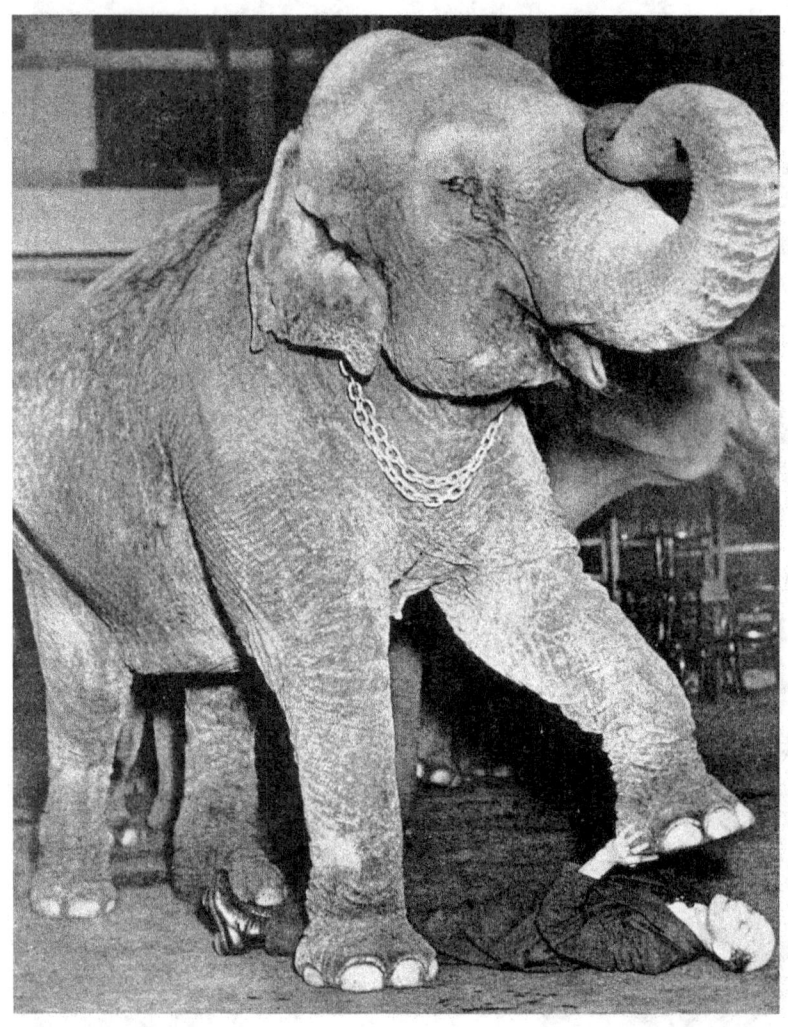

14 The Author and 'Jenny.' She is sixty-five years old and weighs four tons, but her heart is pure gold

same work in Glasgow. Such was the early career of a distinguished Royal Academician.

Abraham Saunders, a protégé of the elder Astley, wandered the country with his circus and, after varying fortunes (he, too, was in prison for debt) fell into extreme poverty through a shipping disaster which robbed him of his stock, and through the burning down of his theatre (the Royalty). He became proprietor of a 'penny gaff' and died miserably poor in his ninetieth year.

When Saunders was at Bartholomew Fair in 1801, one of his boys performed a tumbling act dressed as a monkey. This was a favourite turn with the mountebanks of medieval times. The same boy walked the tight-rope and tumbled somersaults on horseback. One night he fell from his horse and damaged both legs. His circus career abruptly ended, but he became the greatest tragedian of his age: Edmund Kean.

It is in 1807 that we first meet with the name of Hengler—at Astley's, of course. He appears as a tight-rope celebrity. By and by we find Edward Henry Hengler at Astley's when Ducrow took it over, and later joining Price & Powell's circus. The Henglers appear thick and fast; there are several sons and daughters; Charles, however, is the founder of the family fortunes. He had the business head, left artistry to others, and established circuses in Liverpool, Glasgow, Dublin, Hull and Birmingham. In 1871 he obtained possession of the old Palais Royal in Argyle Street (London) and converted it into a hippodrome or Cirque Hengler. The site of this famous circus is now occupied by the Palladium.

When the first Hengler performed there were innumerable circuses on the road. The most celebrated of these were Saunders', Holloway's, Samwell's, Milton's, John Clarke's (he had not even a tent but pitched in an open field), Wild's, Bannister's and Cooke's.

Who this first Cooke was I am not sure, but George Cooke appears in a double tight-rope act at Astley's in 1828, his partner being the rope-dancer Miss Woolford, who later married Ducrow.[1] William, James and Thomas Cooke all made circus

[1] Thomas Cooke was Astley's junior by ten years. He came from an aristocratic stock.

ASTLEY'S
ROYAL AMPHITHEATRE,
WESTMINSTER BRIDGE ROAD.

Proprietor and Manager, Mr. WILLIAM BATTY, Amphitheatre House, Bridge Road, Lambeth, Surrey. Licensed by the Lord High Chamberlain.

Under the Patronage of Her Most Gracious Majesty the QUEEN, H. R. H. PRINCE ALBERT, &c.

The New and Costly Decorations
Of the interior of the Theatre have been designed and executed by Mr. C. NORWOOD, of Hoxton.

Immense Hit of the Easter Spectacle!
OVERFLOWING HOUSES!
Hundreds have been nightly unable to gain admission to witness Mr.

VAN AMBURGH
IN HIS
WONDROUS PERFORMANCES!
Who has on each representation been hailed, with an **enthusiasm unparalleled**, by the most brilliant and **Crowded Audiences** ever assembled within the walls of this Theatre.

EVERY EVENING,
Until further notice, the curtain will rise at Seven o'clock precisely,

To the **entirely New, Grand and Romantic Spectacle**, written expressly for the occasion by BAYLE BERNARD, Esq., the incidents of which have been suggested by a passage in EUGENE SUE's celebrated Novel of

THE WANDERING JEW,
And will be presented under the title of

MOROK

AN EARLY VICTORIAN ANNOUNCEMENT FOR
'ASTLEY'S AMPHITHEATRE'

THE BEAST TAMER!
IN WHICH
MR. VAN AMBURGH
Will appear with his
UNEQUALLED COLLECTION OF
Trained Animals

Among which will be found one of the greatest novelties ever seen,

A BLACK TIGER!

The first ever known to mingle in a group with other animals, and has hitherto been considered **Untameable**, but which Mr. **Van Amburgh** after the most untiring exertion has succeeded in training.

The **Spectacle** has been produced with entirely **New Scenery, Machinery, Costumes, Music,** and **Decorations**, on a scale of **Unprecedented Grandeur!** under the exclusive direction of **Mr. W. West**.

The part of Armand Dugard, afterwards Morok the Beast Tamer, by **Mr. Van Amburgh**.

☞ For particulars of this highly interesting Spectacle, see Full Bills.

The Spectacle will be succeeded by an incomparable routine of BATTY's

SCENES OF THE ARENA,
IN WHICH THE
BRITISH & FOREIGN ARTISTES

Will appear in their extraordinary and elegant

Equestrian Performances!

The Scenes of the Circle enlivened by the Drolleries of the unrivalled Jesters, M. ROCHEZ, Grotesque, and Mr. ADRIAN, the celebrated Provincial Clown. Riding Masters, Signor CHIARRINI and Mr. WIDDICOMB.

The Entertainments will conclude with a
LAUGHABLE FARCE.

Stage Manager - - Mr. W. WEST,
Late of this Theatre, and from the Theatre Royal, Drury Lane.

Box Office open daily from 11 till 5. No remuneration to Place-keepers.
Box Book-keeper....Mr. JOHN.
ADMISSION :—STALLS, 5s. DRESS BOXES, 4s. UPPER BOXES, 3s. PIT, 2s. GALLERY, 1s. UPPER GALLERY, 6d. Children under Ten Years of age, Half-price to all parts of the House (the Upper Gallery excepted). Second price at half-past Eight, as usual. Doors open at HALF-PAST SIX; Performance to commence at SEVEN o'clock.

MATSON'S Omnibusses to Greenwich, and the "Atlas Association" ditto to Paddington, at the termination of the Performance, every Evening.

J. W. LAST, Steam Press, 59, West-street, West Smithfield.

THE ANNOUNCEMENT CONTINUED

history at Astley's, after Batty's management, by their marvellous feast of horsemanship. The Cookes are among the circus aristocracy, the most famous members of the family being John Henry and his cousin Alfred Eugene. John Henry Cooke established a permanent circus in Edinburgh when Hengler came to Glasgow. The pair made a solemn compact in which each undertook to respect the other's territory. This was religiously adhered to—Hengler's never opening in Edinburgh nor Cooke's in Glasgow. John Henry Cooke died in Edinburgh in 1917 survived by his three sons, Leicester, Alfred and Clarence. There is a belief in the family, shared by my friend Dr. John Bulloch, a learned genealogist, that the Cookes were descended from the Earls of Leicester and that the name was once Coke, hence the uncommon christian name of Leicester Cooke to whom, by the way, I am indebted for many kindnesses. Ducrow, Batty, Van Amburgh and William Darby (Pablo Fanque) all established circus traditions but left no permanent memorials.

Wild animal performances were now introduced, and as travelling menageries were immensely popular in the early nineteenth century, the two forms of entertainment were often combined. The most celebrated of these combinations was that owned by George and John Sanger. George was the last proprietor of the ever memorable Astley's. He made a success of it with his circus, after it had almost ruined Dion Boucicault, who had attempted to run it as a theatre. George, afterwards 'Lord' George Sanger, was a circus Napoleon of whom more will be written later.

Twenty-three years after the opening of Astley's, Rickett's introduced the circus into America. One of the Cookes sought his fortune there with another, but soon returned to London. The greatest of all showmen, that great but genial liar and humbug, Phineas T. Barnum, was to combine later with James Anthony Bailey, the organising genius, and produce the 'Greatest Show on Earth.' The Ringling Brothers took it over after Barnum's death and it is still the greatest circus in the United States.

Germany, home of many great circuses, wild-beast trainers, and superb artists, is indebted to the Briloff family. It was in

15 Lord John Sanger's Chariot drawn by forty horses four abreast. From an early photograph

16 Lord John Sanger

17 Lord George Sanger

their modest establishment that the first Renz performed, and Renz to-day is one of the magnetic names in circus history. But so too are Hagenbeck, Busch, Krone, Sarrasani and Strassburger, some of Germany's circus *élite*. They do not travel the Continent only, but take their shows all over the world. The recent tour of Hagenbeck's circus and menagerie opened in Japan and after a stay in India came home via Egypt and Spain.

When one recalls the names alone associated with circus foundations abroad—the Gautiers, Knies, Carre's, Wirths, Salamonsky's, Krembsers, de Bachs, Chiarinis, Schumanns, Boswells, Tournaires and Franconis, the mere thought of attempting a circus history appals. The circus is a microcosm of the most complicated kind. Many of the names mentioned are unknown to Britons, but our circus families are quite numerous. Bostock, Ginnett, Cooke, Hengler, Pinder, Paulo, Yelding, Fossett, Sanger—these are dynastic names, the founders long since dead but the dynasties still flourishing. Many a name appears upon a modern programme which was announced to the audiences of a century and more ago. Achievement in some form of artistry will be sustained through succeeding generations, for inherited ability is more marked in the circus and theatrical professions than in any other walk of life. This phenomenon, for such it is, is possibly due to the intermarriages which have knit so many circus families into a definite kinship. The Cookes, for example, are connected (by intermarriage) with the families of Boswell, Chadwick, Cole, Ginnett, Krembser (German), Lockhart, Macarte, Powell, Shelton, Wirth, Woolford, Austin, Clarke, Crockett, Cruickshank, Franks, Pinder, Sanger and Yelding.[1]

The circus was founded by men who lived in a prolific age. The first Cooke had nineteen children; the first Knie, a tight-rope walker of 1784, had but four sons and one daughter, but one of the sons was performing on the rope at the age of seventy years and had procreated thirty-four children.

I know one member of the fifth generation of Knies, a boy of sixteen, who for some years has been the youngest exponent of high school riding on the Continent. Were this child of the fifth generation to set himself the task of tracing the

[1] Genealogical table, *Cookes*, J. M. Bulloch.

matrimonial connections of his ancestors and their nearest relatives, how long would it take him?

I once made an heroic effort to get what the Americans call a 'straight line' on the Sanger family. As a small boy I was on friendly terms with 'Lord' George, and I am intimately acquainted with most of his and his brother John's descendants. George the Third, who is married to Poppy Ginnett, helped me considerably, but even he was wrong in one particular.

'Lord' George, who was killed by a lunatic in 1911, had no sons but two daughters, Topsy, who married a Coleman, and Harriet, who married Arthur Reeve. John Sanger, who adopted his brother's self-bestowed title, had three sons and one daughter—John, George, James and Lavinia. Of these, James and Lavinia (Mrs. Peter Hoffman) are still alive and active. The second John had six sons; the second George had one son and one daughter—George and Victoria. James has one son, Edward.

James, the present head of the family, conducts the business side of the 'Lord John Sanger Circus' to-day. He is assisted by his son Edward, his nephew Leslie (son of John the second), and another nephew, George (son of George the second); George's sister, Victoria, performs in the ring with her husband James Freeman (Pimpo the auguste). Dagmar, daughter of the second John, is married to another artist, Anders Pederson, trainer of sea-lions. Her sister Ida is not with the show but travels with her husband, Charles Judge, who trains and exhibits chimpanzees. There are members of the family, not connected with the profession, in both Britain and America, and I know that at least one granddaughter of the first George is living in London—Maria Sanger Reeve.

Her celebrated grandfather was an extraordinary character. I remember him as a short, square-jawed man with shaggy eyebrows and piercing eyes. Brusque in manner, jerky in movement and domineering in speech, he was one of those men whose very masculinity is exploited to impress. He had the audacity of the courageous and the courage of the audacious. He aligned himself with the peers of Britain without asking anyone's permission, and defied anyone to rob him of his self-conferred title.

The story is told in his memoirs, *Seventy Years a Showman*, but the whole story is not there. I recount it here for the benefit of a generation puzzled whenever they see the old caravans enter their town. It was from the lips of a noble Lord, during my membership of the House of Commons, that I heard of the abortive effort to deprive him of his 'title.'

In the 'eighties of the last century the American showman, William Cody (Buffalo Bill), brought his spectacular 'Wild West Show' to England. George Sanger met such formidable opposition by featuring wild west tableaux, etc., in his ring and calling them 'Scenes from Buffalo Bill.' The indignant Cody applied for and obtained an injunction against the Britisher, who complacently ignored it, and was duly arraigned for contempt of court. Sanger did not appear, but on reading through the evidence he was irritated at the reiteration of the phrase 'Hon. Mr. Cody' used by Cody's counsel. Suddenly he banged the paper down and roared, 'Damn it! If he's an Honourable, I can go one better than that, and from now on I am a Lord.'

He won the case, and immediately repainted his caravans and wagons with the celebrated sign, 'Lord George Sanger.' This much the reader will find in the old man's memoirs, published in 1910, but he does not complete the tale. The funniest part of the story has never been in print.

People actually believed him to be a peer of the realm. Patrons to the circus increased. Posters and programmes were printed with the new headings, and the showman 'Lord' was discussed wherever the show passed or pitched. Some of the great ones at Westminster gravely discussed the matter, too. They were for taking steps to have this misuse of a noble dignity ended, but some peers, fortunately, possessed a sense of humour, and nothing happened. Many years later, when 'cook's sons and duke's sons' were fighting the Boer War, the question of Lord George's title cropped up again, but the old boy had a trump card up his sleeve.

His circus had visited Balmoral in the year 1898 at the request of Queen Victoria. The following year she commanded it to visit Windsor. After the circus performance the Queen, accompanied by Sanger, visited the menagerie and asked many questions. In every instance she used 'Lord' when she addressed her guide. The artful showman took full advantage of each occasion by prefixing his reply with, '*If it please your Majesty.*'

The conversation ran somewhat like this. *Queen:* 'Pray, what is this, Lord George?' *Sanger:* 'If it please your Majesty, that is a spotted hyena!'

When these Royal command visits caused the subject of Sanger's 'title' to be resurrected, the old showman grinned and said, 'Let 'em try and take it away. If I am "Lord George" to the Queen herself, I don't care a damn *for the rest of the nobility.*'

He would have fought like a demon against any interference, for George was schooled in a tough age. His hard early life had taught him the supreme virtue of believing in himself.

Another name, honoured wherever circus folk foregather (the four corners of earth), is Bostock. Bostock & Wombwell's menageries, and combination circuses and menageries, were surely the best known in all the world, for they travelled the roads of Britain, the Continent and South Africa for one hundred and twenty-six years. Associated more with the wild animal business than the circus in the early days, these historic show-folk will figure largely in subsequent chapters. Enough has been written on origins and antiquities, though one fain would continue. Let us now look at the circus of the twentieth century—on tour.

18 Willy Schumann, 'Whimmy' Walker and Bertram Mills

19 Two Prospective 'Lion Tamers.' 'And still they gazed and still their wonder grew . . .'

20 Equestrienne and Ballerina in an American Circus

II
SAWDUST AND SPANGLE-LAND

IN days of toll-bars and vile roads in the mud of which one's wagon could sink axle-deep, the touring circus proprietor fought a stiff fight. How stiff it was may be learned from the memoirs of E. H. Bostock and George Sanger. Brains, perseverance and pugnacity were the essential qualifications of the showman, for he had to combat a league of enemies. Local authorities did not like him, ugly crowds sometimes threatened him, the very elements tried at times to defeat and ruin him. However carefully he might plan his itinerary he could never be sure of success. Rivals would cut ahead of him, obliterate his advertisements and steal business by forestalling him at some coveted pitch. Strikes and lock-outs in large industrial areas, especially in mining and textile areas, compelled him at times to make detours at enormous loss. The outbreak of an epidemic sometimes meant the abandonment of the tour after an enormous outlay upon new properties, animals and features.

The showman of even fifty years ago lived in that old world of bad roads, steel-tyred wagons and stinking naphtha-flares. He had to have the energy and courage of the older sea-dogs to pull through. Some, alas, went to the devil and injured the profession. Others became content to serve under the more prosperous. Prosperity was born of character, here as elsewhere. People say to me, 'Do you remember Lord George Sanger?' Shall I ever forget him! I met him but twice. He wore a frock-coat and silk topper. He looked to me like a lord, though I had never seen a lord. I was but seven years old in the year 1893. That was the year of the great coal strike in Yorkshire (where I lived) and of our late King's wedding. The veteran was talking business to my father, and he appeared to me to be angry. His voice sounded like the roar of a lion, or like the Cornish ogre's in *Jack the Giant-Killer*.

By and by the angry gentleman stopped shouting and looked at me. Instead of being in a bad temper he was really in a good one. He asked my name and my age and some questions about my school, and gave me a coin. It was the first sixpence I had ever possessed.

I was told by my parent that he was Lord George Sanger, and I believed it. I did not know who Lord George Sanger was. But I knew next day.

The school I attended, at Castleford, closed at noon so that we could see the Sanger procession. Closing the school saved a lot of sin commission. Scores of good little boys and big boys were saved the necessity of telling a pack of lies next day.

The streets were thronged with eager-eyed citizens. I was fortunate, for the great spectacle passed along our street, and the upstairs windows were level with the tops of the caravans and animal wagons. First came six big elephants, followed by clowns and augustes who capered and somersaulted on the cobbled roadway. An heroically attired ringmaster, mounted upon a magnificent Andalusian bay, followed, his steed high-stepping, snorting and champing as a true picture-book war-horse ought to do. He was followed by the mighty chariot containing the band, a huge construction with massive wheels, drawn by a multitude of horses three abreast. The vehicle itself outshone anything on wheels. Its gold glittered in the sunlight, flashing from the crowns of angels, sirens, Neptunes and mermaids disporting around its sides among the foamy seas and palm-fringed coral rocks.

On an elevation high above the driver, a beautiful lady (she was beautiful to me) sat like Britannia on the penny. She held a shield painted like the Union Jack in her left hand, and a gilded trident in her right. A huge Greek helmet crowned her blonde head, and beside her, chained to a strong ring, sat a living lion. The lady was nervous; she did not like the lion, for it yawned every now and then and showed its fangs.

After the chariot came the cages of the wild beasts. The shutters were down, and behind the bars lions, tigers, bears, wolves, hyenas and monkeys either danced around or lay in attitudes of dignified indifference. Between each wagon grooms led some of the larger beasts—zebras, camels, llamas and an ostrich—all in more or less gorgeous trappings of red, green and silver.

21 'The Old Order Changeth—

22 —Yielding Place to the New'

23 Bertram Mills' Circus

24 The 'Lay-out'

25 'The Lions starve at Naples.' The Sale of Captain Schneider's Circus

26 Hagenbeck's Circus

27   A Live 'Tractor'

28   Hoisting the Big Top

This kind of thing is not permitted now, but old folks will remember it. It was a brave and handsome bit of publicity, and brother John Sanger knew the value of it as well as brother George. Every kiddie who watched that great free show became a pest until he or she had seen the circus and menagerie. But everyone went to Sanger's, as they went to the older show, Bostock & Wombwell's, for the visit of either was an event.

I did not see Lord George again for five years. My wandering family had migrated to another county. One day I saw the posters and remembered the noisy little man with the silk hat. When the tent was up and the wagons placed, the more harmless creatures were merely corralled behind low canvas walls. I was here, there and everywhere during the erection of the show and, as usual, got damaged.

A pelican gave me a severe rap with its huge bill for trying to touch it. Bellowing blue murder I was taken into a caravan and attended to by two men and a woman. They were busy tying up my finger when the familiar face of Lord George appeared above the lower half of the door and the volcano erupted. After yelling the men's heads off for 'dawdling' he inspected my hand which had bled somewhat, and tied his own handkerchief around it. This time there was no sixpence. Instead, I was told to stay away from the animals or somebody would feed me to the elephants.

I never saw him again. I did not want to, for I was scared of him. The later Sangers who remember him tell me they were as awed by him as I was. George was one of those beings born to have his own way. He believed he had two superiors in the entire cosmos. One was Queen Victoria, the other the Almighty himself.

Since those far-off times the world has been mechanised by electricity and petrol, and though the spirit of showland is unaltered and apparently unalterable, the outer forms are changed indeed. It is the age of *organisation*, which counts more than does mere forceful leadership. The circus proprietor like Mr. Bertram Mills is still a brilliant commander-in-chief, but he does not lead his troops on a charger, with baton upraised. He sits at the general headquarters in Dorset Square —and draws maps. He covers half the globe every year in a search for talent. He and his two sons, Cyril and Bernard, are as unlike as men can be in character, but the combination of the three has worked wonders for the circus. Every summer they take their little world of canvas, rope, wood and steel, with its human and animal population on a tour lasting for some seven months at least. It is Olympia under the Big Top with the trimmings shorn. But no longer does it crawl horse-drawn along green-flanked, but atrocious, roads. It simply 'arrives' at the pitch, once known as 'tober,' where the great king-poles of the huge marquee await their burden of Greenock cloth. A special train, one of three, stands in the siding at the goods station not far away.

The 'last performance' finishes at 10.30 p.m. The vast audience files out of the gigantic tent unaware that many of the animals, properties and traps they watched so intently but an hour ago have already been loaded behind the steaming engine. Long before the last member of the public has left the showground, an organised army is at work dismantling. The next performance is at 2.30 p.m. on the morrow—thirty or more miles away, on the spot where our majestic king-poles await their burden of canvas. Sleep, but little of it, is snatched by the fortunate few whose duties end early on moving-night. The canvas city is uprooted in three hours, is borne afar to its new halt, and is rebuilt in four and a half hours.

Last of all come the cages of the wild beasts and the other animals. Three hundred men, under direction, draw forth the tools and properties, and long before the first animal has arrived the six-ton mass of amorphous canvas has spread around the steel masts and is being rapidly guyed and walled into the centre of all circus activity, the Big Top. Ten tons of iron stakes and as many miles of ropes harness it to the ground.

While one work-gang—labourers, grooms, artists and proprietors—busy themselves here, another is erecting the tent for the stables and menagerie, while others are journeying back and forth to the railway depot unloading the animals and bringing them up to the pitch. Under the canvas the ringmaster superintends the cutting, measuring and preparing of the ring. If the surface is too hard it is broken up by pickaxes, and over it is distributed one or more cartloads of soil.

29 Dressing Room: Percy Huxter, Harry Coady, Dolly and Milly Sloan

30 Dressing Room: The lovely Lai Foun Girls

31 A Thousand Electric Bulbs festoon the great tent of Bertram Mills' Circus

The ring-fence is erected, the tan and sawdust sprinkled over the soil to form graceful arabesques, and the ringmaster, giving his approval, retires to draw up his time-table.

Meanwhile, some forty or fifty wagons and caravans, tractors and trailers, have been grouped around the great tent, each in a spot selected by design. There is meaning in the very disorder of circus-land. Alleyways, gangways and open spaces give access to the workers and animals which now begin to arrive. They come in instalments, some led by the tapes and some saddled and ridden by groom and performer.

White Lippizans and Arabs, conscious of their aristocratic lineage, the essence of grace and symmetry; chestnut, roan and sorrel stallions with the pride of Andalusia in every step; cream-coloured Anglo-Russians, pied and skewbald mustangs from America, spacious-crouped half-breeds of Belgian and Portuguese descent, ponies from Tartary, Exmoor and Shetland, mules from the Argentine, and those horses that are not horses, the hogmaned, stripe-arrayed zebras from the African hills and plains. Liberties of felicitous movement and delicate precision; equine Pavlovas of the *haute école*, dignity expressed in every sweep of the tail; and rosinbacks—the humble, homely, lovable horsefolk, but the very core of the performance even as they were its origin.

They come silently as ghosts, for the brutal iron nailed to the hooves of their less fortunate fellows is absent here. The delicate *laminae* of horn have not been brittled and parted by the application of red-hot shoes. The marvellous natural arch of the hoof and its mechanism of resilience remain unspoilt. They take their stalls strewn with wholesome straw, the elasticity of their beautiful bodies disclosed by every movement.

At the end of the elongated tent forming the stables is a large wooden platform cleared for the elephant hobbles, awaiting the arrival of the four Indian comedians, Julia, Roxie, Jenny and Lena. They weigh anything between four and five and a half tons, have prodigious appetites, and range in age from eighteen to sixty-five years.

Here they come, tiny eyes twinkling above the swinging but ever-restless trunks, sober as the 'lords or ladies of unnumbered days' ought to be—until they reach the temporary *keddah* on the showground. They stroll to the limits of the field, beyond which an interested crowd watch, and cadge for whatever trifles may be forthcoming. There are no beggars on earth superior to elephants. Soon they have separated, each investigating with its serpentine nose-hand the impediments encountered on the stroll.

And now for a phenomenon of training not starred, as it might be, on the official programme. The four gigantic brutes have wandered away from each other, and they are wanted for hobbling. They have to perform in a couple of hours' time. Their master stands in the centre of the compound, and with startling suddenness runs swiftly to a spot some twenty yards away. As he runs he calls their names, and calls them as though he were in deadly danger. Four trunks are erected skyward, their owners wheeling upon their hind legs with the speed of kangaroos, a raucous trumpeting rends the air, and the four living tanks thunder towards their beloved trainer and range themselves shoulder to shoulder like good soldiers before him.

A moment's drill for discipline's sake follows the salute—trunks on high, right feet raised—and at the word of command they file with the gravity of philosophers into the stable, mount their platform, receive their hobbles, and begin again their gustatory exercises. The elephant's feeding-time begins when it is born and ends when it dies. It is subjected to many interruptions—that is all.

The stables are now in order. Upon the stall-posts hang the gay trappings of the occupants. Grooms are busy polishing sleek hides and diapering the rounded croups. They whistle and sing, but must not smoke under pain of dismissal. Opposite the horses, across the gangway, the wild-beast cages have been coupled in one row. Fifteen rufous forms, black-striped and white-bellied, march backward and forward, each awaiting its twelve pounds of well-blooded meat. The great masked faces from which glare red balls of fire are framed in white ruffles. There is no face on earth quite so magnificently terrible to gaze into as the tiger's.

Feeding-time is near, and every beast exhibits the excited impatience of the cat kind. Roar succeeds snarl as partitions are thrust through the cage divisions, and, when the trolly appears, each of the painted beauties becomes a jungle fiend once more—ears laid back, sabre teeth exposed, claws distended to grasp its joint of well-blooded meat amid an inferno of spits and growls.

In a little while they will rush to the great steel arena and perform graceful evolutions at the bidding of a mere man. They will growl at him and strike at him, for that is their nature. They simply cannot help it. But they have no desire to hurt him, for he has never hurt them. He worships them as he would worship his own children. But may the good Lord have pity upon any man who places himself at the mercy of a tiger or lion to whom he has been cruel. While the animals are feeding let us enter the Big Top again. Transformation! The furniture is all bolted together and draped, and arc lamps swing forty feet above; private boxes encircle the ring, and the programme girls, costumed, have taken up their places. The entrance gallery facing the quickly gathering crowd is filled with neat-uniformed bandsmen. The pay-box is open, and the queue has gathered.

A great engine throbs. Two thousand electric bulbs festooning the big tent flood the exterior with coloured light. Down in the caravan alleys there is much activity. Grime has been removed from strong bodies; property wagons, now empty, have become dressing-rooms; paint, powder, fleshings and elaborate costumes lie on improvised tables in apparent confusion. Men who were swinging sledge-hammers an hour ago are swinging grease-paints before a mirror.

Pass along these 'dressing-rooms,' and you will hear some eleven different languages. Like its animal population, the human element in the circus is gathered from earth's four quarters. Here are equilibrists from China and Japan, aerialists from America, stock-whip manipulators from Australia, perchists from Italy, contortionists and tumblers from France, cowboys and vaqueros from the U.S.A. and Argentine, risley acrobats from Russia, wild-beast trainers from Germany and Czechoslovakia, and dwarfs, midgets and clowns from fairyland itself.

Dainty equestriennes flutter by like *prima ballerinas*, strong men are tautening their muscles behind the curtains, stilt-walkers are climbing ladders to their stilt-levels, labourers are bolting together the sections of the 'runway' along which the lions and tigers will come to enter the caged ring. Weird gadgets are being sorted out and laid behind the curtain at the performers' entrance, and artists in fleshings and bespangled brocade are carefully scrutinising the wires, bars, nuts and bolts prior to their call.

They have already submitted the fittings within the dome of the tent to the minutest of tests. Every circus performer who exploits his muscular agility above ground must be perfectly trained in body and mind. Especially does this apply to the artists of the flying trapeze, the Roman rings or the steel perch.

Precision, judgment, balance and strength are the essentials of the performer, and the appurtenances must be fitted together with almost hairbreadth precision. The Angel of Death occupies a front seat at every performance, and the artiste knows it. The sagging of a rope through atmospheric influence might throw a trapeze-bar out of adjustment and bring disaster to the intrepid performer, so particular care must be observed.

The well-tested props are collected together, and beside them, with eagle eye, stands the ringmaster. He has exchanged his plus-four suit for a jacket of vivid scarlet, black trousers and silk topper. He is now the 'Equestrian Director.' He blows stridently upon a whistle, waves his white gloves, and a crowd of 'ring-boys' group themselves near the mysterious properties.

Above the main entrance the bandmaster faces his men and raises his baton.

A fanfare from the brasses and a roll of drums reverberate over the waiting and expectant multitude. Gates are slipped and curtains drawn from the painted entrance. 'Red tickets to the right, blue to the left, white tickets straight ahead!' Pass into the cleanest, bravest and cleverest entertainment on earth.

32 'Allez Oop!'

33 A Close-up of the Medrano Sisters, Resitta, Anita and Wanda

III
CIRCUS HORSES

'CUT the cackle and come to the horses,' said Andrew Ducrow, a phrase that has become common currency. Contrary to popular belief, circus horses are not bred specially for the ring. When they are not of pure Kehailan blood they are overwhelmingly Arabian, for liberty horses, and these are in the majority, are selected for beauty and symmetry as well as for intelligence. The vivid description of an Arab mare in the Abu Zeyd cycle of tales will fit equally well the stallion of the circus:

> *Spare is her head and lean, her ears pricked close together,*
> *Her forelock is a net, her forehead a lamp lighted,*
> *Illumining the tribe, her neck curved like a palm branch,*
> *Her wither sharp and clean. Upon her chest and throttle*
> *An amulet hangs of gold. Her forelegs are twin lances;*
> *Her hoofs fly forward faster ever than flies the whirlwind,*
> *Her tail-bone borne aloft, yet the hairs sweep the gravel.*

The slim Trakehners and stately Lippizans[1] are more than three-quarters English thoroughbred, and from these the liberty groups are mainly selected. The noble horse is a noble horse no matter where bred or who breeds him, and on one occasion my friend Bertram Mills crossed a field to examine a horse at grass, negotiated the purchase and included it in his group of Trakehners. Something sturdier is required for the high school (*haute école*) acts, and the so-called Andalusian barb, a mixture of barb and Fleming, is a favourite mount. It has good bone, a good round barrel and a well set-on tail.

The jockey-act horses are known as 'rosinbacks,' and they may be anything. I have seen a Suffolk Punch and a light Belgian vanner used in the ring. Any horse with a well-rounded croup, not too heavy, but with a spacious back will

[1] Called variously Lippizanas and Lappizaners—from Lippiza, near Trieste, where they were originally bred for high school riding.

make a rosinback. They are incredibly docile and the best-tempered creatures in the circus. Before entering the ring their backs are sprinkled with powdered resin to afford a grip to the performer's feet. In early days this was not required, for the 'pad' was used. The bare-back is much to be preferred, for the ungainly pad not only spoilt the appearance of the animal but detracted from the performance of the artist. Many of the astonishing feats performed by the Astleys and Cookes were achieved without the pad, it is true, but the equestriennes of the middle of last century liked a miniature stage on the horse's back.

In spite of distance lending enchantment to the view, our circus artistes of to-day are as brilliant as any in the past. The circus has many competitors in the entertainment world and it is not singled out for special praise. Last century a Charles Dickens, a Richard Harris Barham or a Tom Hood could sit for hours at the circus and write genially about it. To-day the cinema and its pinchbeck galaxies have the special pleaders. Taste has altered, certainly, but so has the circus. Performances are speeded up to-day and the variety is sometimes bewildering. Our riders and trainers do not do so much to-day, not because they cannot, but simply because taste has changed. Yet it is safe to say that every act of the past is being repeated in some circus ring in some part of the world.

The circus began with the horse, and the horse is still the pivot of its existence. No horses, no circus. The automobile has almost abolished the horse from our streets, and the younger generation, who regard it as a 'back number,' know little or nothing of the horse-trainer's art.

Perhaps the most celebrated trainers of the past were the Schumanns (it was said of the original Schumann that a wooden horse would obey the crack of his whip), but the Schumanns of to-day are every bit as clever as their forebears. In Britain our best trainers are all foreign at the moment. The Dutch Carre Family, the two Kossmeyers, Albert Jesserich and Czeslaw Mroczkovski are the best known. A brilliant trainer of recent years, Captain Ankner, has returned to the Continent. These men are all amazingly clever exponents of trick horsemanship as well as great trainers. Many of them,

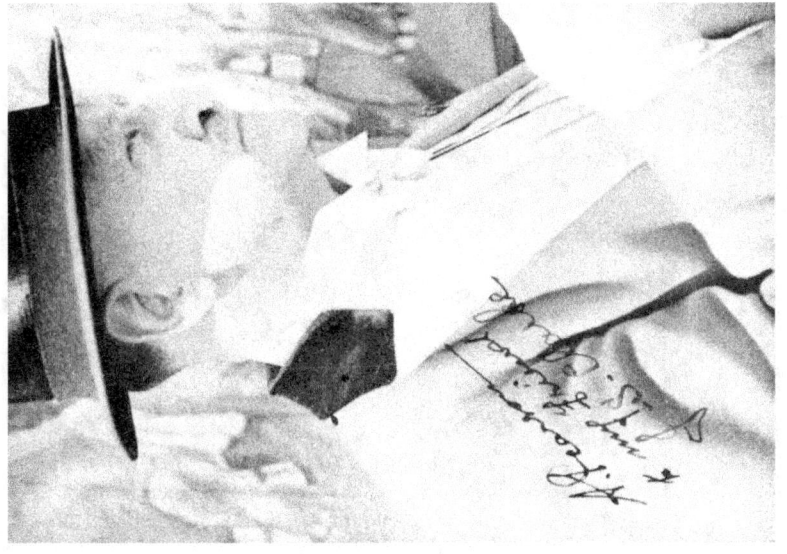

34 The Kossmeyers: 'High School' Exponents

35 The Veteran

36 Canvas Stables

37 Training Liberty Horses

38 Mroczkovski with Castor and Pollux

39 Training a Girl 'Courier'

40 Czeslaw Mroczkovski. His mount is a magnificent Lippizana Stallion

however (I exclude Mroczkovski), are disciples of another celebrated Englishman who established a new technique last century. He was James Fillis, son of a London barrister.

When Baucher excited our early-nineteenth-century forefathers with his high school horses, few people thought improvement possible. *L'haute école* had definitely arrived and was, indeed, the backbone of circus equitation. Then came James Fillis—the nearest approach to the mythical Centaur that ever was. Fillis was unique in his day, for his performance was more than amusement. It was not only an exhibition of superb horsemanship but a demonstration of animal-human 'mutualism.' What the spectator saw was not a series of stereotyped movements governed by rein, crop or spur, but a marvellous co-ordination between man and mount, almost telepathic in essence.

Fillis had spent many years in the study of equine psychology and equine anatomy. He not only knew the mind of the horse, but had an intimate knowledge of every muscle and sinew in its body. Horse action and reaction were, to him, an open book. He embodied his observations in a treatise on the art of equitation which is still the classic of circus riders, though few of them have the time to obey its injunctions to the letter. In it he wrote:

'The highest perfection of the art of equitation, and the ideal for which every rider must strive, is a constant, and complete, mastery over every action of his horse—not merely over its lateral movements.

'When that is achieved, we see two living creatures welded into perfect harmony, and the rider becomes so much a part of his steed that he can sense all the impressions it receives; they can reach his brain so swiftly and surely that his every action accords harmoniously with a responsive action of his horse; the latter takes their mutual understanding for granted, adapts itself to his will, and so attains complete agreement with his intentions.

'From that moment onward, the horse's actions are purely reflex, for between the two of them there is only one brain—the rider's.'

This treatise, *Principes de Dressage et d'Equitation*, was written by Fillis at the behest of the late M. Clemenceau. It became the Bible of Horsemanship to hundreds of trainers and performers, and is still discussed wherever circus men foregather.

Fillis, it will be seen, did not believe in a rider imposing his will upon the horse. He was a pioneer of animal psychology to whom a horse was not merely a horse, but a creature with a peculiar sensitiveness and an individuality. This, not generally recognised, is what distinguishes a creative rider from the 'mechanical' trainer.

There is a great danger of this important truth being lost sight of. In many high school performances to-day the horse is made to execute the stilted and altogether ugly movements of certain modern dances. These are so entirely artificial that harmony between mount and rider is impossible. The animal in its jerks and shuffles looks like an automaton—a clockwork horse—while the rider sits with a strained look as if anxious for the number to finish. There may be cleverness in the preparation of such acts but they lack the chief essential of art—beauty. Equine dances of a similar character are distinctly pleasing when the animal is at liberty. Mroczkovski, for example, a grand trainer and a magnificent showman, recalls certain of his liberty horses and, by merely waving his whips, gets them to dance the most intricate steps *while the music keeps time to the horse*. Thus an original brain turns modern ugliness into almost antique beauty. Whether Phillip Astley's two horses in the famous 'minuet' act were liberty horses or not, we do not know. If they were not this must have been the first high school act in circus history. The French 'hauté école' is, therefore, misleading. As an essential circus number it has always been popular, and modern critics who draw comparisons between our present-day exponents and those of the past forget one inconvenient truth. When Baucher, Fillis, Mounet and their disciples were entertaining former generations of circus fans and arousing the wildest enthusiasm by their prodigies of horsemanship, time was not the important factor it is to-day. These men had time to burn, and they spent it in the training of their animals. They sometimes trained a horse, before showing it, for four years. Our trainers

42 Arix

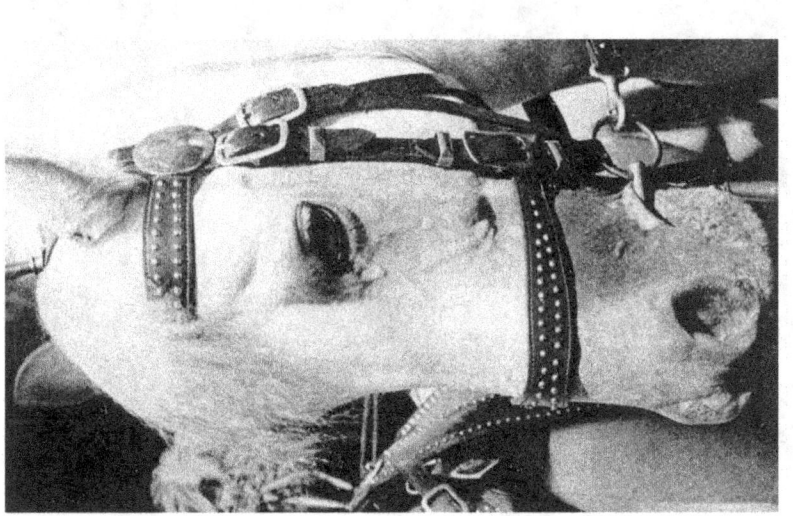

41 Patience

Two of Bertram Mills' Liberty Horses

43 'Courier of St. Petersburg': Amy Huckle

do it in exactly four months, and the result is almost as perfect.

Arthur Velasco gives a marvellous performance without even a bridle on his mount. Arturo Manzano, Harry Carre, Alphonse Kossmeyer, Baptista Schreiber, Michaela Busch, Albert Jesserich, the two Petolettis, Oscar Fischer and Helmuth Barth have all given most excellent exhibitions in Britain within recent years and sometimes under difficulties that would have appalled the giants of last century. This is the era of speed, and no slackening is permitted once the performance has commenced. Act must follow act in rapid succession—every artist strictly timed by a table drawn up by the equestrian director. The circus is as rigorous in this respect as the B.B.C. There is, moreover, a serious curtailment of rehearsal time owing to the multiplicity of acts. The high school showmen of to-day are really very wonderful people, and if Dr. Kober[1] is correct in avowing that Burchardt-Footit and Thereze Renz are the only two left to carry on the Fillis tradition, I can only reply that any falling off in quality to-day is due to the problem of time, not to lack of genius. Personally, I cannot see the deterioration except in the 'mechanical numbers' I have mentioned. I deplore these, not only because of their infelicity of movement, but because they most assuredly strain unduly the delicate mechanism of a horse's legs.

It might be argued that the special bits, bridles, spurs, reins and other controls and guides such as the crop, the knees and the voice used by modern *haute école* exponents make his task a mechanical one in any case. That, unfortunately, is true in many instances, but there are superb artists who dispense with these. In 1931-2 Olympia patrons saw Julio Viaz de Valesco perform his high school act without bridle, bit, reins or switch. This modern artist, who received his training at the hands of the famous Canero, created an act unknown even to James Fillis. A fellow Spaniard, Arturo Manzano, who toured Britain for some years, was justly admired as a graceful performer and a trainer of genius. He had a peculiar disposition and did not get on too well with his fellow artistes, but every one confessed to his amazing skill and ring personality.

[1] *Circus Days and Circus Nights.*

II

Of circus horse-folk, the rosinback is the most homely, lovable and certainly the most romantic. Often but not invariably plebeian in origin, it wears any livery—black, brown, roan, sorrel, white, chestnut, bay, piebald or skewbald, dapple or 'flea-bitten.'

It is always safe and always intelligent. It *began* the circus and without it the circus is unthinkable. That it knows its job thoroughly, the very few accidents which have befallen its human co-partners will testify. The various acts performed upon the rosinbacks are too familiar to require detailed description. They are usually called 'jockey' numbers and 'high voltige,' and consist of the customary posing, tumbling, dancing and somersaulting with the horse pacing or cantering around the forty-five foot ring. All manner of novelties have been introduced into the act, a favourite one, performed by equestriennes as a rule, being the handkerchief trick. In this a number of handkerchiefs are placed upon the sawdust and plucked by the rider who careers around the ring while suspended upside down from the girdle of the horse. Two very popular acts which lost favour for a time but are now on every programme were 'jumping the balloons and garters' and the delightful *Pas-de-deux*. The 'balloons' are the tissue-paper hoops through which the equestrienne jumps, and the 'garters' are the broad maypole streamers held by clowns who swing them under her feet as she leaps from her mount. In the *Pas-de-deux*, two horses are used, one performer swinging his partner into graceful poses while he strides the two trotting animals. There are many variations of this act, which are frequently burlesqued immediately after by the clowns.

The most beautiful performance to-day is that of the three Medrano sisters, who perform upon three horses and employ a steel horizontal bar for some of the acrobatics. This exquisite act deserves detailed description, for the public do not fully appreciate the extraordinary cleverness of it all. While two of the young girls stand upright upon their mounts, holding the bar across their shoulders, the third sister, from the back of the centre steed, leaps upward, grips the bar and

44 'Pas-de-Deux'

45 'Jumping the Balloons'

performs a series of acrobatic feats, concluding by standing balanced upon the slender rod as the three horses trot round the ring. While balanced in this way, a difficult enough feat when the bar is a stationary one, this young lady has to adapt her mind and body to several different movements. The horses are moving rapidly forward, their backs are rising and falling, and the bar itself rests upon the shoulders of two living beings who have to adjust their movements with the

LUCIO CHRISTIANI'S SOMERSAULT

movements of their horses. This almost incredible feat is not only performed with success but with a grace and beauty charming to behold.

One of the most astounding jockey acts is that presented by the Christiani family. There are seven of them, five brothers, and two sisters. Anything that was ever achieved upon or from a horse's back is child's play to the Christiani's. Notari and his beautiful sister Machaquita present the *Pas-de-deux* with skill and refinement, and Lucio in clown's costume burlesques it in most amusing manner. Lucio is a wonder—one of those rare circus artistes who succeed in doing something for the first time. His solo act is the most daring one in circus history, and has, as far as I know, never been successfully achieved by another horseman. He leaps first from the ring and lands upright upon his horse's back, from which he turns both forward and backward somersaults. He repeats this with his ankles bound together by a handkerchief. Another horse is brought in by a groom, and as the two career around the ring, Lucio throws a backward somersault, and, while doing it, *passes a hoop over his body* and lands upon the croup of the second horse. A third horse is brought into the act, and the three trot around, not head to rail, but neck to flank.

Twice round the ring, then Lucio, with a glance behind, throws a somersault and lands upon the back of the third horse. Such a feat had always been regarded as impossible.

When the Christianis came to this country, a special leaflet describing Lucio's trick, written by myself, was issued to the public, whose lack of appreciation was due to perplexity rather than coldness. Spectators saw an incredible feat performed but did not understand it. A backward somersault from one horse to another is not difficult (to an acrobat) *when the animals are stationary*. In Lucio's trick, however, there are the complications of several kinds of motion to contend with. *The three horses are trotting forward, their croups are not rising and falling in unison, the somersault is not a clear backward one, for the horses are not in Indian file, the acrobat flings himself sideward as well as backward, completes a cycle with his body and lands erect upon both feet upon a moving platform (the third horse) which actually progressed during his passage through the air.* It is synchronisation brought to perfection. The public was not slow to appreciate after the difficulties were explained, and Lucio 'brought the house down' at every performance.

As an example of how distance lends enchantment to a circus act as well as a view, read the old-time descriptions of Andrew Ducrow's novelty known as the 'Courier of St. Petersburg.' Ducrow introduced this always pleasing number at Astley's in 1826, and took the Londoners' breath away. It was described as 'unparalleled and stupendous' and 'the last word in daring horsemanship.' Ducrow had perfected a combined jockey and liberty act. He dashed into the ring standing upon two horses, and during his circlings four horses galloped in succession from the vestibule and passed between his outstretched legs. As they passed below him he stooped and snatched a white ribbon-rein until, to the 'utter amazement' of the audience, he was soon seen to be straddling two horses and driving four more tandem-fashion.

46 The Medrano Sisters again. Anita will stand upright on the bar while the horses make a circuit of the Ring

47 The Baker Boys

48 A Schumann Number

49 The Loyal Repenski Group 'Corinthian' Act

50 Liz the Mare and Billy Baker: the simultaneous jump

51 A Grand Carousel at Olympia. This superb spectacle, in which seventy human and equine performers form concentric circles in the Ring, is seen best from above

Up till last year a slim, delicate and very pretty young woman of twenty years, Miss Doreen Blackbourne, was performing this 'courier' act at Bertram Mills's circus with twice as many horses as Ducrow used. She straddled three horses and drove nine others. At Hagenbeck's Circus young Fred Petoletti, son of the famous horseman Karl, uses thirteen horses and, at times, seventeen. He strides four horses all going at a brisk trot and drives five pairs. The seventeenth horse is at liberty, and lifts the act out of the commonplace by pirouetting most daintily in the lead.

This is the age of speed, noise and crowds, and the solo riding act of old, unless the artist is a particularly clever and equally beautiful equestrienne, is no longer popular. Groups who perform their specialities in turn and wind up with a finale in which six or seven riders leap on to the one horse are more in favour.

III

The liberty act can be good or bad, that is, beautiful or ugly, but it is always spectacular. It is good when the horses, all highly spirited entires, are well trained and work in a proper ring. For some years we have had the deplorable stage-circus with us, an abomination at best, where the centre of activity, the ring, is restricted to some twenty-four feet. It is utterly impossible to manœuvre even twelve animals in so limited an area with pleasing effect. A good liberty act is not only true circus but a crowning achievement in the art of training. The horses are taught their rhythmic evolutions by an elaborate process which demands a high degree of skill on the part of the trainer, to say nothing of the enormous expenditure of nervous energy and an almost superhuman patience.

A group may consist of twelve, eighteen or twenty-one animals circling, wheeling, dividing, coupling, tripling and quadrupling at the whispered word of command or the crack of the whip. Their movements are correlated into an harmonious ensemble, and their step and carriage must be of a given quality. Few animals excite the admiration of mankind to the same degree as a group of liberties when entering the ring from the curtained vestibule. Their arched necks and stately trappings augment their natural lissomeness and superb contour, and their every movement appears full of dignity. The arched neck is due to the bearing-reins which draw down the head and keep the animal under control. 'Cruelty!' shriek the critics, who forget the miseries of labouring horses and the bearing-reins of aristocratic carriage-horses of former days. Cruelty? Was ever a horse, or any other creature, maintained and cared for as these proud animals. That bearing-rein is necessary when many horses work together. It maintains order and protects the horses themselves from one another. Stallions, however well-trained, are still stallions, and a full-sexed horse can be very dangerous. The discomfort of the side-straps is borne for some quarter of an hour, two and sometimes three times a day. It is almost negligible. The rest of the time the animal is at ease in comfort and even luxury. The stables are spotlessly clean, the incessant grooming gives an obsidian-like sheen to the hides, and nothing but the most carefully selected fodder is given to the circus horses. An aristocrat in pedigree and a perfectly trained one at that, the liberty horse is too valuable to treat cruelly. It is not even shod, for shod horses would be a source of danger to the public. Liberty acts are liable to become stereotyped and new arrangements are continually sought after. One of the most pleasing acts is toured by Hagenbeck's in which blacks, whites and browns, all perfectly matched, group themselves in colours *en suite*, then in alternate colours, then in odd doubles and trebles. The trainer smokes a cigar, never utters a word, but does everything by snapping his fingers. It is one of the most effective numbers I have seen. Sometimes spectators are in doubt as to what is actually taking place. Fred Petoletti's liberty group, after their more familiar gyrations and groupings, are permitted to stroll around until they are apparently hopelessly mixed up. Every animal carries a silver-plated number and there are twenty-one of them. When the whip is cracked they fall in line and trot in disorder. Round and round they go, Petoletti in the centre remaining perfectly passive, and in less than four

52 Manzano at Olympia

53 The Kossmeyers' *Haut-école* Duet

54 Outside the Ring: The Medrano Sisters

minutes every horse has found his proper place in the circle, the numbers running consecutively from one to twenty-one. The pomp and circumstance alone of a good liberty act runs away with a lot of money. Bertram Mills has a stud of twelve cream-coloured Lippizans who, under the tutelage of that young but magnificent showman and trainer, Mroczkovski, perform every number in a liberty repertoire, and were dressed in trappings which cost £75 per horse. Last season they appeared in a new number adorned in simple white belts and tapes. Nothing finer than this act has been seen in a modern circus.

IV

UP IN THE DOME

AERIALISTS, those daring and graceful men and women who achieve seemingly superhuman feats in mid-air—forty, fifty and sometimes seventy feet above the circus ring—are among the elect of the circus world. They resent the intrusion of the net in Britain (insisted upon by law) because it detracts from the marvel of their performance. The net, by the way, is to protect the spectator from injury or from shock following an accident. If a performer falls into it he is as likely to break his neck as if it were not there.

There was no net stretched below Emile Gravelet, better known as 'Blondin,' when he stood upon his head, wheeled a man in a barrow blindfold and cooked an omelet on a stove, on a tight-rope crossed over the Niagara Falls. Blondin's kind comes once in a century, but to-day the Concellos, Codonas (American), Alberty, Hegelmanns, Wallendas and Colleanos are little removed from him in sheer wizardry. The Lawrence Sisters, the Vesses and the Wortleys perform the seemingly impossible on suspended bars and vertical rods, while Cubanos, a Dutch artist, defies death every time he climbs into the dome of his tent or solid structure.

These performers never intrude their art; the public remain quite ignorant of it. That is because the circus makes no appeal to the intellect—it is pure entertainment.

If the aerialist, for example, was at all concerned about 'how' he did his work, instead of concentrating upon doing it—he would more than likely break his neck or back. Nevertheless, he, or she, is a superb artiste, though few people think so.

In a 'flying trapeze' act like that of the Codonas or the Concellos, there are two 'leapers' and one 'catcher.' The catcher hangs upside-down, either gripping the trapeze ropes with the legs or hanging from his hocks (the inside of the knee-bend), with his feet in a 'cradle.' The leapers stand on

55 In this, as in every Aerial Act, nerve, judgment, precision and timing must be perfect

56 The Triple-in

57 Winnie Colleano in the Heel Swing

58 The Flying Pass: Catcher to Catch

59 Aerialists making ready in an American Circus

60 The Flying Concellos. Three of the World's greatest Aerialists awaiting their Call

the spring-board fixed to the king-pole. One grips his trapeze bar, and, at the word 'Go,' throws himself forward. At the third swing he releases his bar in mid-air, turns a triple somersault towards the catcher and is cleanly caught at the wrists.

Meanwhile, as the two bodies swing, 'leaper number two' grips the bar, throws himself from the spring-board and 'flies' through the air towards the catcher. The swinging catcher releases his partner and catches the second leaper. The released partner, the first leaper, twists his body in mid-air and, catching the trapeze just vacated by the second leaper, swings on to the spring-board.

The spectators are daily thrilled at this hair-raising feat, but cannot grasp its implications. They do not realise that the entire series of movements have taken about ten seconds to perform; that the flying figures each weigh about eleven stones and that, during that astonishing ten seconds, an enormous muscular effort has been exerted; that three brains have worked in perfect synchronisation, calculating distance, time and equilibrium with absolute precision, and that every bodily organ and every nerve of each performer is kept in tune by rigorous self-discipline and continual practice.

Besides all this, however, there are risks which must be taken, however careful the artiste may be and however perfect his judgment. Between two performances in a tenting circus the atmosphere may alter. Rain, fog, even the heat generated by a thousand warm, breathing bodies, will influence structural fittings and affect appliances.

Arthur Concello is the only living artist who can do the triple somersault now that Codona has retired. He is teaching his wife, Antoinette, who performs with him, to do it and she is making rapid progress. Antoinette is one of the most perfectly proportioned women in the circus world and certainly one of the most courageous.

The flying trapeze act, with double, two-and-a-half, and an occasional triple somersault, as well as double passes, is performed in America by the Clarkonians. This act always has been the most popular one with circus patrons, for it is that rare combination, grace, beauty and talent, brought to the highest degree. One of the finest trapeze artistes of last century was Alfred Eugene Cooke, the brother and partner of John Henry. The Cookes were noted for their handsome forms and features and 'Gene' was well favoured with the family heritage. He became the hero of the most popular song of the day—recently resurrected with some success.

> He floats through the air with the greatest of ease,
> That daring young man on the flying trapeze.

In these acts the performers actually develop an instinct or sixth sense by continuous association. The 'timing,' from the moment the leapers leave the bar, pirouette or somersault in mid-air, and extend their hands to the catcher, is, and must be, absolutely perfect. The difference in the fraction of a second means death or disaster. The three minds become 'tuned in' to one another, and the bodies respond to telepathic influence. That is why the withdrawal of one partner breaks up the act. The reflexes upon which so much depend would not function if a substitute were used, unless he or she had 'understudied' by equally continuous practice for years.

Sometimes tragedy of a more sinister kind destroys a great circus act. I once knew the Three Sylvains. Two of them, brothers, are dead. It happened this wise. The third partner of this almost incomparable trio was a girl who joined the group after their erstwhile partner had become permanently disabled through a fall. Everything worked smoothly until the brothers discovered they were both in love with their co-worker. No one was to blame. So far from playing one off against the other, Helena, the girl, tried her very best to maintain a strict impartiality. During an entire tour the two brothers refused to speak to one another. The younger one, Dolf, vacated the living-wagon, and took lodgings at every halt. Jealousy kept the fires of hatred ever smouldering, and an incessant brooding turned the hitherto light-hearted brothers into the bitterest enemies. At every performance the three went up into the dome and completed their act, bowing their

61 'Luisita' in the Neck Hold

62 The lithe bodies swing sixty feet above the Audience

acknowledgments when applauded and smilingly taking their call at the conclusion.

When Wilhelm let go of his trapeze-bar and pirouetted towards his enemy brother, he had no fear. He always knew those strong arms would be waiting and that those sure strong wrists would be at the right spot to clutch. The 'act' was everything; it subordinated everything; it belonged to the public and to the circus. Left to brood alone in his wagon, however, Wilhelm took to secret drinking. His nerve remained unimpaired, but his judgment went awry, with ghastly results.

They carried him from the ring with a broken back, and next morning Dolf committed suicide by swallowing some powerful disinfectant. The act was ended for ever.

Five years ago I met Helena working solo as a butterfly, spinning suspended by her teeth from a strap fifty feet above the ring. I drew the conversation round to the tragedy then eighteen months old.

'Poor boys,' she said. 'I think of them with great sadness, but I have to forget them up there!' She pointed to the dome—to remember them there would be to invite disaster.

Equally daring and clever are those who perform on the high wire; they are true descendants of the rope-dancers or flyers of olden days. One of these, Cadman, is depicted in the act of descending his rope in Hogarth's painting of Southwark Fair; he was subsequently killed when sliding down a rope at Shrewsbury. Another slack-rope artist figures in the same picture. Frost tells us his name was Violante, and he married a woman named Lupino, an ancestress of the modern theatrical family of that name. No rope-walker ever equalled the exploits of Blondin (Emile Gravelet), a Frenchman born in the village of Omar in 1824. Possibly no human being ever possessed so uncanny a sense of touch and balance as he did. Apart from this essential of his craft, he was one of the most daring and confident men who ever lived. It is a curious fact that Blondin could do most circus acts requiring nerve and skill, but he never excelled in horsemanship. He was an accomplished gymnast on or above the ground, but rope-walking was second nature to him. He repeatedly crossed Niagara Falls on a rope stretched some 170 feet above the chasm, he wheeled a man over in a wheelbarrow, he carried a stove into the middle of the rope (1,000 feet in length) and cooked an omelet above the deafening cataract. Blondin performed all over the world and always attracted huge audiences. He appeared in England in 1861 at the Crystal Palace and at the 'World's Fair' at the Royal Agricultural Hall, Islington, some forty-five years ago. John Swallow, who directs the circus at the Agricultural Hall, told me recently that the staples to which Blondin's rope was attached are still *in situ* there, and 'Pimpo,' the celebrated Auguste of Sanger's, assures me that he was born in a caravan in the same hall during the performance of Blondin. One of the most hazardous feats ever attempted was his passage along a rope some 430 feet in length stretched between the main and mizzen masts of the P. & O. steamship *Poonah*. This was in 1875, when the ship was steaming at 13 knots and rolling somewhat heavily to boot. Twice he had to sit down when a swell lifted the ship, but though several passengers fainted, he never once lost his nerve during his double journey between the masts.

A few Chinese contortionists and tumblers introduce variations of rope-walking, but to-day the high and low wire acts have ousted tight- and slack-rope performances from favour.

Dare-devils of the dizzy heights who juggle with their own bodies and sometimes the bodies of their partners are the perchists and pole aerialists. Nothing can be more graceful than a perch act, such as that of the Walkmirs or Oliveras. The perch of resilient steel, weighing some 150 pounds, is balanced upon the shoulder or forehead of the 'carrier.' The 'top-mounter' climbs to the top, and from this precarious position assumes various classical poses, alternating with gymnastic feats. Though very pretty to watch, the act is really dangerous. The top-mounter in the Olivera troupe broke his neck some eighteen months ago.

Pole aerialists like the Vesses perform in concert from thin masts forty or fifty feet high. Outdoors they think nothing

63 A Close-up of the Wallendas. The two centre figures are not yet mounted

64 The Terrifying Wire Act of the Wallendas

65 Alberty on the Swaying Pole

67 A Close-up of Alberty on his Fifty-foot Pole

66 The Vesses perform at an elevation of seventy feet

of standing upon their heads at the top of slim steel poles seventy feet above the earth. The young lady of the troupe carries off a 'stunt' which never fails to freeze every backbone in the audience. All eyes are riveted upon the slim beautiful figure of the girl who balances herself on the apex of the pole. She stands upon her head and thrusts out her arms; she places her feet in leather hoops and poses with her body taut at right angles to the pole; she mounts upon the shoulders of her partner and balances herself upon her head with his head for a platform.

Suddenly she slips, and with a piercing scream falls to the ground, seventy feet below. Half the audience jump to their feet in horror; the other half close their eyes in sickening anticipation—but nothing tragic has happened. The little lady is hobbled at the ankle, and she swings laughingly at the end of a sixty-foot rope.

Now, this is not easy, for she would dislocate a leg were it not for the perfect arc she describes when falling through the air.

'How do they do it?' asks the reader. They have been doing it since they were five years old. They have developed and co-ordinated brain and muscle by persistent practice until the top of a swaying pole is to them what a street pavement is to you.

Accidents do happen—they cannot be avoided by the cleverest. The simplest feats have been perfected at the cost of life and limb.

An amusing fellow that clown—is he not? He was not always a clown, but the greatest aerialist of his day—but disaster overtook him.

Young Alberty, son of the celebrated trapeze-artist, sways upside-down from the top of a steel pole fifty feet high. He has fallen on two occasions. I massaged him one night after the performance and found a swelling upon his leg as big as a duck-egg. His father is a picture of grace in the air, but outside he limps. He is permanently lame—the result of a crash sustained through a slight discrepancy. He struck the king-pole instead of the spring-board and fell some distance to the ring. Not having had time to rehearse before his appearance at this particular circus he took it for granted that his apparatus was in order. It *was* all in perfect working order, but the trapeze-bar and the spring-board had been fixed for a flight of 14 metres.

Alberty always worked for a flight of 16 metres, and on this occasion *his precision* nearly cost him his life.

68, 69 Successors to Blondin. In Tight-rope and Tight-wire Acts gracefulness is but one Essential

70 Auguste and Clown: C. Mayer and T. Delfin

V
THE CIRCUS SPIRIT

WHEN the circus fell on evil days, the music-hall claimed many of its brightest stars. Among these were Grock, the clown, and Lehmann Kara, the juggler. Lehmann was a dear friend of mine, who toured the halls under the magic name of Paul Cinquevalli.

Not even Rastelli was a greater juggler than the handsome Paul. He was an agile and perfectly formed miracle of precision in pink fleshings and glittering sequins—a true descendant of those fair-haunting mountebanks who tumbled, juggled and contorted, before Rahere, the minstrel, 'got religion' in the days of Henry I, and began the Fair of Saint Bartholomew.

Cinquevalli was the idol of every artist. He held a glass in his mouth containing a billiard ball; upon the ball he balanced a cue; on the top of the cue he balanced two billiard balls, one on top of the other. He had a cannon-ball weighing nearly half a hundredweight, which his assistant flung across the stage to him. Cinquevalli caught it beautifully on the edge of a small plate. The heavy iron ball, a billiard ball, and a celluloid 'ping-pong' ball were juggled with as neatly as the ordinary juggler juggles with balls of the same size and weight. Cinquevalli usually closed his performance by having the fifty-pound iron ball drawn up to a collapsible shelf forty feet above the stage. His assistant then pulled a cord, and the heavy ball released from the shelf, was deftly caught upon the neck of the juggler.

From beginning to end of Cinquevalli's act there was not one tiniest scrap of trickery. He practised his more sensational numbers for eight years before 'putting them on.'

At the first performance one night at the Newcastle-on-Tyne Empire, the plate upon which he caught the ball broke in his hand. His fingers were severely cut and the ball rolled on to his right foot, clad only in fleshings with a flexible sole. Cinquevalli went through his performance at both 'houses' with his fingers frightfully lacerated and the toes of his right foot a mass of pulp. The audience were quite oblivious of anything more serious having happened than the breaking of a bit of crockery. They had not been let down through the 'indisposition of the artist.' That is the spirit of the circus star, whether he performs on the stage, under the canvas dome, or under the open sky.

I have experienced this a score of times, and have always had to smile when I read of the 'temperamental' film star or stage beauty.

Romanticists who know little of the circus hinterland have invested the clown with a mantle of melancholy. His mask of grotesque farce hides the tragedy writ large upon his face. Pure moonshine! The wailing, whining Canio of *I. Pagliacci*, deploring so stridently his misfortunes while donning the motley, is a good theme for the dramatist and storyteller, but nothing like him ever happened in circus life. Trials and tribulations, heartaches and despondencies afflict acrobats, jugglers and animal trainers as well as clowns, but none of them is ever guilty of unloading his or her miseries upon the public. The ring-fence which separates performers from spectators under the great tent is not so insurmountable as that higher ring-fence of reserve which divides them outside.

One of the most exacting of professions, the circus breeds stoicism in its children. What is known in other artistic circles as 'temperament'—really a neurotic hysteria induced by an overplus of vanity—is virtually unknown there. Whim and caprice is there in abundance, but never in such form as to interfere with the act.

Sandwina, mother of Teddy, the boxer, was, until recently, the strongest woman in the world. She carried her husband around the ring on her extended palms; she lay on a bed of spikes while blacksmiths hammered an anvil upon her chest. She caught huge shells and cannon-balls upon her neck, and broke chains asunder with her bare hands. One day, accosted by a *roué* when out shopping, she struck him one blow with the flat of her hand, knocked him clean across the street and through a plate-glass window.

71 The pretty Perch-act of the Walkmirs. The Perch is balanced on the shoulder of Ambrose; his Wife is aloft

72 Clowns and Augustes 'Fill In'

To Dr. Kober, the publicist for Sarrasani's circus, she said one day, 'Did I ever tell you what happened to me one night when practising with my cannon-balls?

'I felt slightly giddy and went to my caravan—and how shall I put it—a quarter of an hour later my first-born made his entrance into the world.'

Sandwina was a Brumbach before marriage, and the family had produced both Samsons and Goliaths for some generations. Sandwina's prodigious strength, therefore, was an inheritance; nevertheless, the character of her performance demanded careful and regular practice.

One may argue that the possession of enormous muscular power in a man or woman is a sure indication of lack of nervous energy. This is by no means the case, though the strong folk may be excluded from the present argument. There are grounds for believing that, during their act, circus artistes cease to be human in the sense that they are controlled by their art and not subject to the customary emotions of mankind.

The case of Hopper is a good example. Hopper was an American sharpshooter who performed a 'William Tell' act with his wife. This was a favourite item in the repertoire of S. F. Cody before he took up aviation.

Hopper shot an apple from his wife's head, aiming from the other side of the ring. One afternoon Mrs. Hopper carelessly left a note from a secret lover lying on her dressing-table which her husband had the misfortune to read. Not one word was said in rebuke, not even a frown disfigured his brow, but that night his aim was very poor. . . .

An artist may be ill, brain-fagged or worried by some private affliction. No matter, he will appear in the ring at the scheduled time.

Dr. A. H. Kober of Sarrasani's, himself a man of brilliant attainments who abandoned a profession to become a circus publicity manager, recounts the heroism of Jean Clermont, trainer and exhibitor of dogs, cats, pigs and birds. Jean travelled with Barnum and Bailey's, but in 'off-seasons' appeared in vaudeville as a comedian. On the way to perform at Regensburg his child died in his arms. Jean reached his hotel, ordered a coffin with his heart breaking, and within an hour was bringing shrieks of laughter from his Hippodrome audience. His three-year-old child, following the elders, sent to post a letter, was run over in the street. The child died just before Jean left to fulfil his contract. He provoked as much merriment as usual and returned to his beloved dead.

One night Clermont was awaiting his call in the wings when a telegram arrived announcing the death of his wife. Within five minutes he was on the stage enhancing his reputation as a fun maker. Clermont is still performing.

Many patrons of Olympia are well acquainted with the very clever voltige act of the Baker Boys. Keen observers would recognise these same whirlwind riders under their American Indian paint and costumes when the Bertram Mills Circus toured Scotland four years ago. I have known three generations of the Bakers, and knew the father of the four boys long before the eldest of them was born. The Bakers had their own circus, but it never reached the spectacular stage. The family concentrated more upon performance than upon business and organisation. Their show, consequently, remained small, but the family adhered to the old circus tradition and reared artistes.

Seven or eight years ago, the small tent of the Baker circus was pitched on a vacant lot at Willesden. The 'star' turn was the jockey act by young Tommy, then about fifteen years old. The little show was visited one night by Bertram Mills and one of his sons who, recognising the talent of the young boy, promptly offered him a contract for Olympia. Thus 'Young Steve,' as Captain Mills renamed Tommy, achieved stardom and fame in a single night. One after another the younger boys, all trained by their father, took their places in the ring until the act was not only clever, but pleasingly humorous. Readers will recall the *finale* when the old white mare, 'Lizzie,' with a strap of bells round her neck, galloped at terrific speed while Tommy somersaulted in company with her round the ring.

At the Kelvin Hall, Glasgow, in 1931-2, the Baker family performed for Mr. Bostock, carrying through their Olympia act without an omission. When the act was over Tommy took his call and crawled as a very bandy-legged clown from the ring. For nearly three weeks young Baker delighted and thrilled thousands of Kelvin Hall spectators while suffering from a slipped knee-cap which he had dislocated during rehearsal. The clown's paint concealed his grimaces of pain, the affectation of bandy legs disguised, somewhat, the painful limp.

Early in 1932 Tommy ran off on the sly and married a fellow circus-artiste. Innate shyness prompted him to this. In September he was on tour in Scotland and looking forward to the winter season at Olympia. Just one week prior to that event he died from an attack of peritonitis—not yet twenty-three years of age. Tommy was one of the kindliest and sweetest-natured of young men, and many of his admirers in Scotland will be pained to know that *finis* has been written to so promising a career.

On the same Scottish tour of the Mills Circus appeared the Wallendas, whose dare-devil act on the high-wire, thirty-five feet above the ring, was a staggering demonstration of human nerve. It might be opportune at this point to remind the reader that in all circus acts where apparatus of any kind is employed, the artistes themselves are solely responsible for the fixing, testing and readjusting of all such apparatus. The Wallendas met with a mishap at Ibrox which might have had very serious results. The supports of the small platform, which held it to the king-pole, broke one night when four performers and one assistant were standing upon it. They were all violently precipitated, but, with the quickness of mind that comes from dangerous living, they clutched at anything that happened to be there—the broken platform, the steel wire stretched over the ring, etc. None of them fell, but two of them, Lulu (the girl) and Willy were injured. Lulu could not perform for some days owing to leg injuries, but the act was one of the sensations of the show and could not possibly be cancelled.

The sensation of the act was Lulu balancing herself upon Willy's shoulders, Willy being seated in a chair balanced upon a rod stretched between the breast and shoulders of Philip and Henry, who in turn carried their delicately poised partner across the ring from pole to pole on a wire thirty-five feet high. After the accident I found Willy next morning nursing a wrist. One of the small bones was fractured. At the performance the Wallendas appeared as usual—all but Lulu. Instead of sitting on his chair Willy balanced it on the pole, gripped both arms and stood feet uppermost, supported by his wrists, one of which was causing the sweat to pour from him in agony. He maintained his position and preserved a perfect equilibrium during the entire passage across the wire. The spectators applauded the feat of daring and its skilful execution, but they knew nothing of the heroism that accompanied it—that was merely an incident in a day's work.

There are two groups of Wallendas performing on the high wire, the second group crossing the wire with the two carriers mounted on bicycles. They appeared in England last year under the name of the Five Carlos, and a tragedy almost occurred one evening when the audience was already in a state of excitement over a mishap to a rider. The cyclists, carrying their balancing rods and supporting their partners in this truly terrifying act, had just reached the terminus when the girl, overcome by the heat in the dome, fainted. Fortunately she fell *forward* from her perch and was seized by the receiver on the platform.

Bertram Mills, who introduced both Wallenda groups to British audiences, told me that he personally cares little for such acts. The sensational is at times artistic, but these almost miraculously sensational feats, however artistically accomplished, cause physical pain in the beholder by the dreadful suspense they create. There are a good many 'sensational' circus acts which are not genuinely so, but good entertainment. Spectacular is the correct word, but the audience is given the impression that deadly danger accompanies their achievement, and an atmosphere of suspense is created which is entirely false. On the other hand, really dangerous feats are performed which have all the appearance of safety and simplicity.

The head of the Allison troupe of Risley acrobats runs across the ring and throws a *double forward somersault from the ground*. He has been doing this for some time, but his body is putting on weight and it is becoming increasingly difficult.

73 *Poses Plastiques* at Blackpool Tower Circus

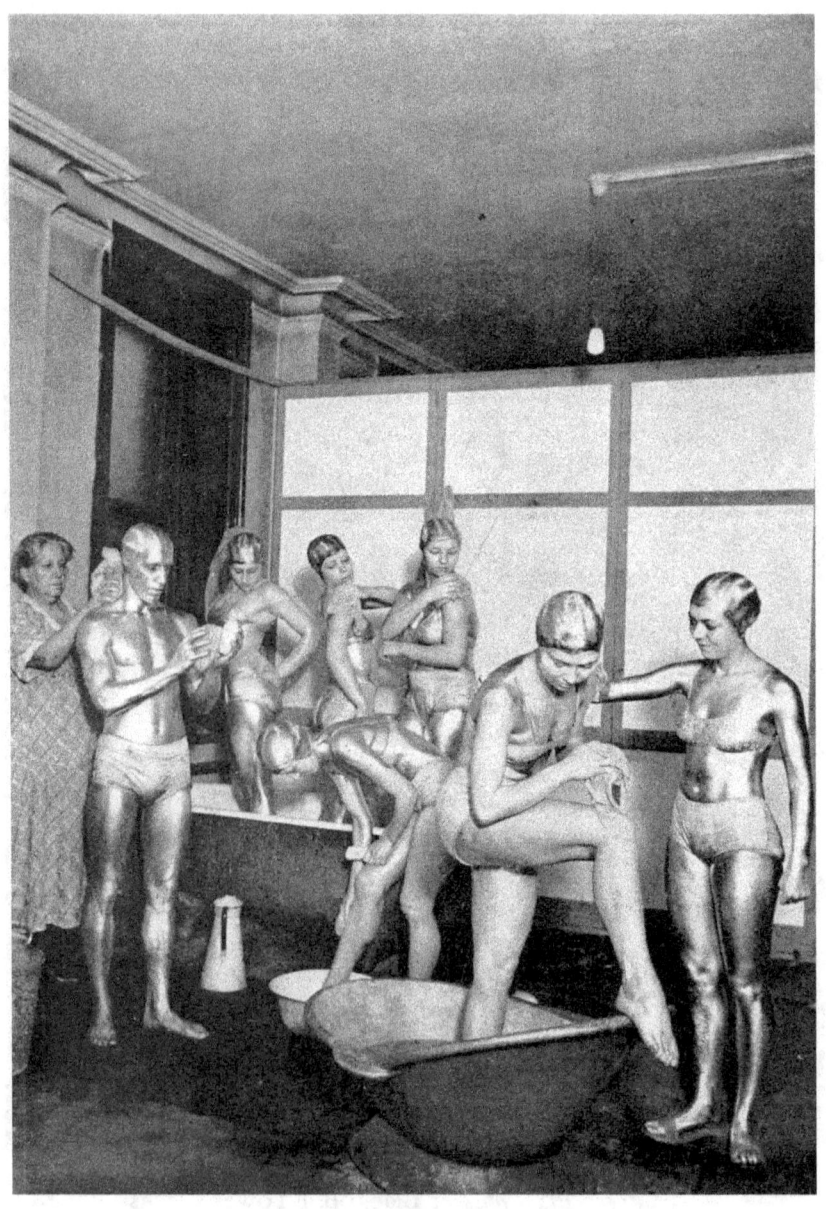

74 The Marcelle Golden Statues. Washing off the Glycerine and Gold Paint

'When do you intend to abandon that trick?' I asked him. 'When I break my neck,' he replied. The public see this feat so rapidly that they do not comprehend either its wonder or its danger. Very few have succeeded in doing it more than once, and many have met their death in attempting it.

It was first accomplished by Tomkinson in the year 1835. *His successors were all killed*—Richard in 1866; Muller in the same year; Bourgeois two years later; Harper, Poposchill (a woman) and Wise in 1889; Ulrich in 1890, and Toner in 1893; Jackson in 1895. Every one of these dislocated the neck. Four men have attempted the triple somersault—Gayton, Hobbes, Amor and Dutton. The first three were killed; the fourth succeeded in doing it—once. Nothing on earth would induce him to attempt it again.

The double somersault in the air is performed in scores of circuses to-day, but right up to the year 1922 the triple somersault was considered quite impossible. In that year the young aerialist, Alfredo Codona, achieved it in America and has done it ever since. It is one of the outstanding thrills of every performance at which the Codonas appear. Alfredo is still in his thirties, but has tasted the bitter fruits of tragedy already. He met, and loved, the happy Lilian Leitzel, one of the cleverest and possibly the most celebrated woman aerialist of modern times. Lilian performed the hazardous body-whirl from the Roman rings fifty feet above the ring. Bathed in a shaft of light thrown upon her costume of fleshings of pink and silver, she executed over one hundred twists of the body while hanging by one hand from the suspended ring. Codona and Leitzel were married in 1928, the union, long looked-for, being celebrated in circus circles as the marriage of the King and the Queen of the air.

The conjugal happiness of the couple was destined to last less than three years. On Friday, February 13th 1931 (ominous day and date to the superstitious) Lilian was performing in the Copenhagen winter circus when the rope upon which she was gyrated gave way and her frail body fell to the ring and was picked up beyond earthly aid.

A touching sequel followed in December, when Lilian's ashes, enclosed in a silver urn, were sealed by Alfredo her husband in a crypt below the statue he had designed for her. Of pure Carrara marble, the statue is of the artist, life-size, being caught in the arms of her husband. An expression of fear sits upon her face as her arms cling to the strong body of her lover. Below the figures, two Roman rings with a broken rope recall the tragic happening at Copenhagen, and underneath is chiselled the word 'Reunion.' Some eighteen months ago Alfredo strained a tendon and performs the 'triple' no more. He has become an Equestrian Director.

Death occurs in the circus like epidemics some years. Three years ago, at the Christmas season, nine favourite stars were killed in different parts of the world—some of them, however, by wild animals. When one remembers the enormous number of performers in very hazardous acts and the number of times they appear each year, the number of fatalities is surprisingly small. Death seldom occurs naturally during a performance. Actors and actresses, both on the stage and in the film studio, die of heart-failure or from some other cause, but in all my experience I have never known this to happen in a circus ring.

Circus artistes are very careless as a rule and less accidents would occur if more attention was bestowed upon the properties.

II

When erected in the ring, the trapeze poles, trampoline, and wire apparatus are always minutely inspected and tested by the performers—but they seldom look afterwards for the effect of wear and tear. Cleeks, swivels, bolts and wires have a knack of wearing out like anything else, and one day the limit of endurance is overreached with unhappy results.

I have known only one fraud perpetrated in the ring during all my thirty-five years' experience. Even here the people were thrilled by an act of dare-devilry and were completely satisfied. A man was shot from a cannon into a net fifty feet distant. Spectators saw a figure climb into the cannon's muzzle, wearing an airman's helmet, they waited breathlessly for the terrific detonation, they saw a human form launched from the cannon's mouth hurtle through the air and fall into the net. It was terrifying and genuine—but it was not the person represented! Two 'assistants' took turns in being shot from the cannon as 'live' shells—the much advertised 'artiste' did nothing but own the ordnance.

One afternoon the net was overshot, and assistant number one was carried from the tent with a broken back. At the evening performance (same day) assistant number two was seriously injured. The circus is not afflicted with much of this kind of thing, fortunately.

I have called this act a fraudulent one because the men who were actually shot from the cannon were not on the programme—the owner's photograph appeared as the star of the performance.

VI
CLOWNS AND CLOWNING

THERE existed a time when the world was without a joke. It must have been during the great Ice Age or before man appeared at all, for man has always had a sense of the ludicrous.

Ancient Egypt had its Trinculos and Merry Andrews, its Grocks and Grimaldis, who entertained the commonalty on feast days in the Sphinx avenues before the great temples. On the vases and urns of Greece one may see delineated not only the tragedians and comedians who bowed to Thespis, but those misshapen ones who begot laughter, often born of cruelty, and who owned Momus, god of Merriment, their Deity. Yet Momus himself enjoyed not mirth; his heart was leaden and his spirit heavy. Chaos was his grandsire: discord and death his brethren.

There was something cruel about early laughter, and its traces linger to-day. The circus clown is a make-believe half-wit, a tragedy in itself, and we laugh at his lunacies perpetrated in the ring of sawdust and laugh louder when he tumbles and hurts himself. Such laughter is significant even though we know that he *doesn't hurt himself.*

Long before clowns there were buffoons. They were usually 'simples' or hunchbacks—living caricatures for courtiers to laugh at. They were kept at court to amuse bored monarchs and, if the monarch was capricious, he not infrequently dispelled his peevish vapours by slaughtering a buffoon or two.

The medieval age was an age of buffoonery and an age of cruelty. The dwarf was a kind of ogre like the giant his opposite, or the fanciful beasts of disordered imaginations, the gryphon, dragon and cockatrice. When the age of reason began to dawn and the sun of knowledge began to penetrate the clouds of ignorance, the 'dark ages' retreated before the advance of an enlightened race.

An appreciation of wit followed, and the witty one rather

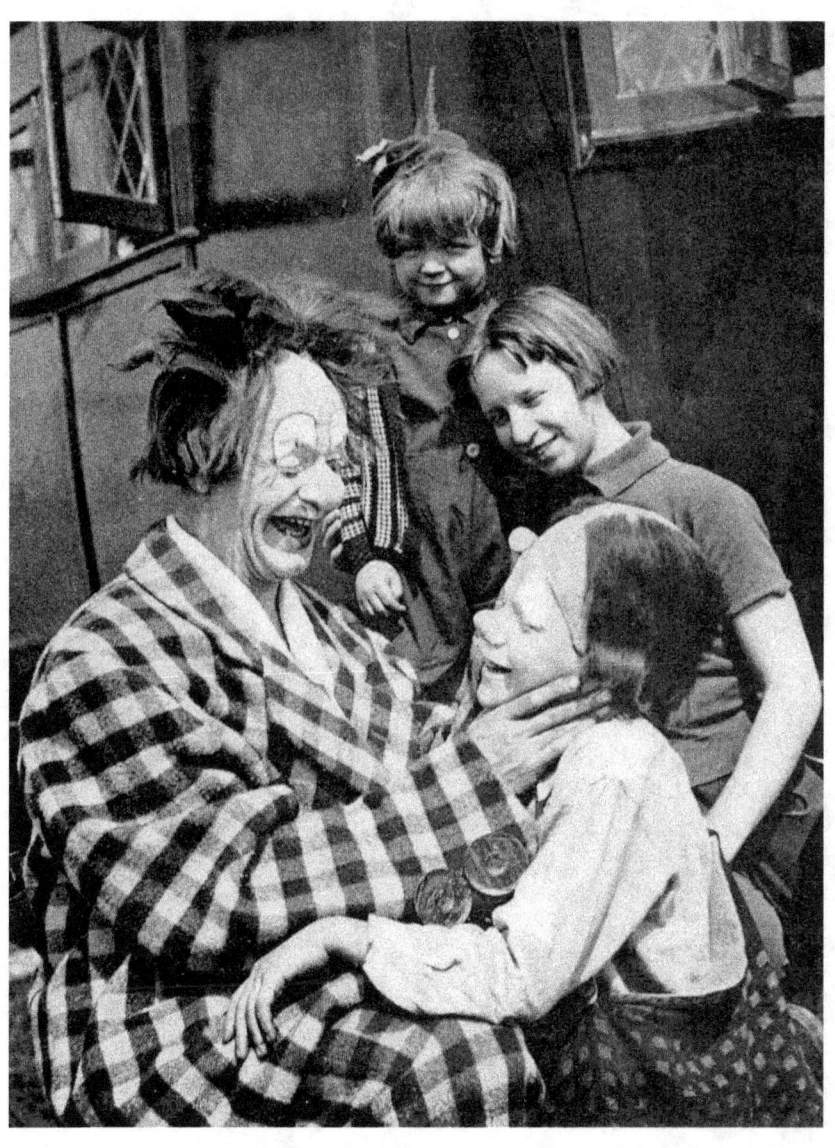
75 Coco educates Sasha

76 'They look before and after,
And pine for what is not . . .'

than the grotesque one was courted for his company. The buffoon no longer lurked behind the throne; he was banished from the regal presence and in his place pranked the forerunner of Yorick, the jester. He held an honoured office and was robed for it. He wore the motley—tunic, tights, and cap and cape, with bells dangling from the scalloped edges of both.

In his hand he carried his wand or sceptre of office, the Fool's Bauble—a rod tipped with a fool's head of bronze or silver with an inflated bladder tied with string to the ferrule. A daring, and often lovable, man was the king's fool. He brought with him the priceless gift of laughter cleansed from the filth of brutality, but still provoked by coarseness and sometimes by the discomfiture of others. But it was a levelling kind of wit he employed.

His windbag smote a head without hurting it and the monarch's head was no exception. His sallies, which 'often set the table in a roar,' were indiscriminate and directed at the corpulence of the throne's occupant as at the spindle-shanks of his chamberlain.

Mankind had progressed, for no one enjoyed a joke against himself until the coming of the jester. So to keep a jester on hand became fashionable. Stately castle and modest manor boasted its jester, who was known at times as the family fool—to distinguish him, no doubt, from the fool of the family. He was immensely popular and his office became one held in high esteem. Merchants used his head as a watermark in their paper, and that paper at the present moment is catalogued as 'foolscap.'

He became less and less of a laughter-maker and more and more of an adviser, until, indeed, he became the special friend and companion of the king. History has preserved the names of many of these peculiar people. We can read of Will Somers, of Scogan, Heywood, Tarleton, Pace, and Archie Armstrong, jesters to many Tudor and Stuart sovereigns.

Archie was jester to James I and to his son Charles I. He was made a free citizen of Aberdeen and remained so until his death. When King Charles went abroad Archie had to accompany him, and he caused some commotion among the nobility of England by demanding a valet like the rest of the members of the royal suite.

There was no fool at the court of Oliver Cromwell. Times were too serious, no doubt. The Protector was not without humour, be it said, and it is gravely recorded how boisterously he laughed at seeing one of his soldiers throw a bucket of water over another. Oliver thought of the fool's bauble when he looked at the Commons' mace. The last man on earth one would have expected to find harbouring a jester in his train was possibly the last 'gentleman' of Britain to keep one—Judge Jeffreys. That jester followed him during his terrible circuit, the 'bloody assize,' and on one occasion he tossed to him the pardon of a culprit so that he might make a little money by selling it to the victim's relatives.

Thus the passing of the jester finishes on a note of cruelty, even as his story began. At Court the Poet Laureate has survived as an office without much profit, but the jester has departed back to those from whom he originally emerged— the common people. You will find him to-day, minus his bauble and his bladder, but still with his merry cry, 'Slap, bang! here we are again!' turning his catherine wheels under the Big Top, and poking fun at the august monarch of the circus world, the ringmaster.

I have indicated the succession of the grotesque character, here, rather than the pedigree of the clown. One must beware of critics—and there are clowns and clowns. Clown means 'clod,' something a trifle higher than the village idiot; one indeed who cannot help acting the fool but can fashion a witticism and be cunning to boot. It was Menander who put him on the stage of ancient Greece, and Phillip Astley who brought him first into the circus ring. The first clowns did not speak; therefore they differed from jesters. The jester ridiculed others, the clown is ridiculed by himself and by others. He is a travesty in the circus as Auguste, but as clown he approaches the clever rascal of Pantomime. *He* may have sprung from *Punchinello*, but the circus clown was originally *Pierrot*.

The eighteenth century saw the culmination of dumb-show in harlequinade—the original pantomime—and the clown was

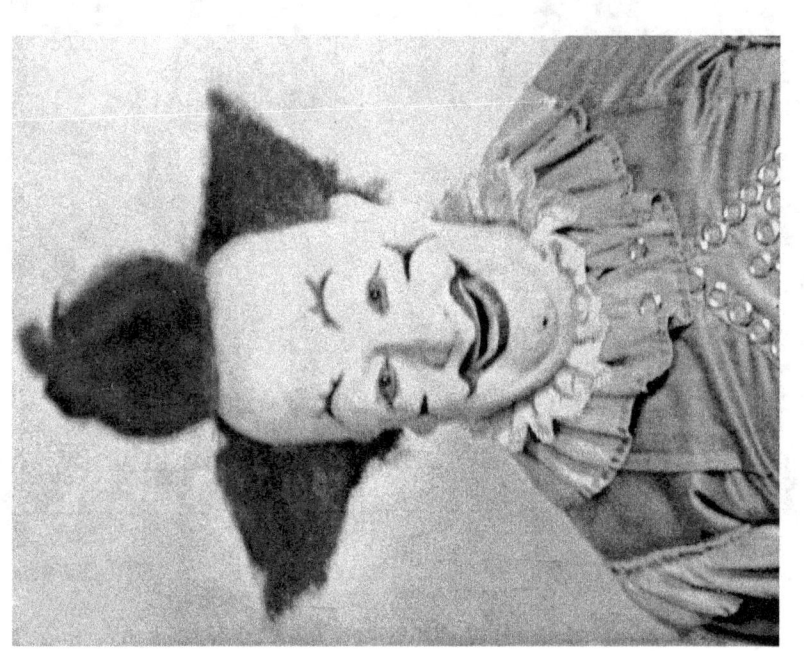

77, 78 Two Studies of Whimsical Walker

79 Circus Parade: Stilts

80 The Sloans are World-famous Stilt Artistes

81 'Charlie': Charles Rivels

added in that century. In the nineteenth the policeman was added. Harlequinade is dead, but the clown still crops up in theatre and music-hall. This theatre-clown follows the tradition established by the celebrated Joseph Grimaldi and he has become confused with the circus clown.

Grimaldi was a clown of harlequinade, not of the circus ring, and he established the 'Joey' tradition. His costume and make-up were copied for a century. Meanwhile the spangled clown of the circus—an entirely different-looking creature to the 'Joey'—tumbled, contorted, or played the fool on horseback or tight-wire, either as an 'entry clown,' or as a 'fill-in' during intervals between the acts. Before the middle of the nineteenth century two new characters made their appearance—the 'grotesque' in the circus and the funny man, known as the 'music-hall comedian.' The ridiculous costume was adopted by some of the funny men of the circus.

When Tom Belling, the famous funmaker, tripped accidentally and sprawled in the ring the crowd roared 'AUGUSTE IDIOT' in derision. Next evening Belling pulled on some baggy trousers, reddened his nose and deliberately repeated the fall of the previous night. The screams of merriment which greeted his antics set the hall-mark of popularity (and permanence) upon the 'Auguste.'

The Auguste is true circus, and so is the *entrée* clown. There is now a fourth type of clown, which arose in our own time. To the 'Joeys' and 'Augustes' we have added the 'Charlies.' It is the privilege and the glory of genius to end something or begin something. To Mr. Charles Chaplin we owe the creation of the pity-inspiring, shabby-genteel little tramp.

To travesty human nature without begetting the smile of cruelty is a great and wonderful art. 'Charley' does it, and he has become as fixed as any of the others. The billowing trousers, huge boots, bowler hat, little cane, and tooth-brush moustache inseparably associated with Charlie Chaplin are found to-day in every part of the world. The 'Charley' is a wonderfully effective combination of the dumb-show actor, the comedian and the circus clown who performs as an acrobat or juggler. I know five amazingly clever circus

'Charlies' including Charley Rivels, who is one of the highest paid fools in the circus ring.

The original Charley—Mr. Chaplin—who helped to keep the whole world sane during the Great War, I know very well. I have met and dined with him several times; on one occasion with Lady Astor, the late Lady Cynthia Mosley and Mr. Lloyd George. This latter was a curious dinner-party, and the topics of conversation were not, as one might suppose, humour, clowning, or even the cinema, but the world depression and how to cure it by the rationing of leisure.

That is one of the curious things about clowning—the seriousness of clowns in private life. Some of them are positively funereal, most of them are ludicrously solemn. One I know spends all his spare moments studying forensic medicine. When performing in Glasgow he asked me to procure for him Professor John Glaister's text-book. Another clever and truly funny auguste of my acquaintance reads every book on political economy he can lay hands upon. He can quote Jevons, Marshall and Karl Marx by the yard, and is argumentative to the point of being cantankerous.

The most famous clown I ever met was Whimsical Walker, who died last year at the age of eighty-three. He was of the Grimaldi tradition and a link with the circus of old. 'Whimmy' became a clown in 1865 with the showman Biddall, who afterwards toured with a ghost-show; he next joined the circus of Pablo Fanque (William Darby). Fanque died in 1871 at the age of seventy-five. Four years later, after several changes, Walker was clowning with the Charles Adams circus. He went to America the same year, returned to Adams shortly after, and joined Hengler's after a short tour. Another visit to America followed, when he appeared in Forepaugh's for a time and then attached himself to Barnum and Bailey's. On his return to England he rejoined Hengler's and it was from there he went, at the request of Sir Augustus Harris, to Drury Lane. Up to the year, if not the day, of his death the old clown was in harness. For many years he appeared at Olympia during the Mills' circus season, riding in the grand procession as Father Christmas seated in the illuminated chariot, and afterwards entertaining the children with his property

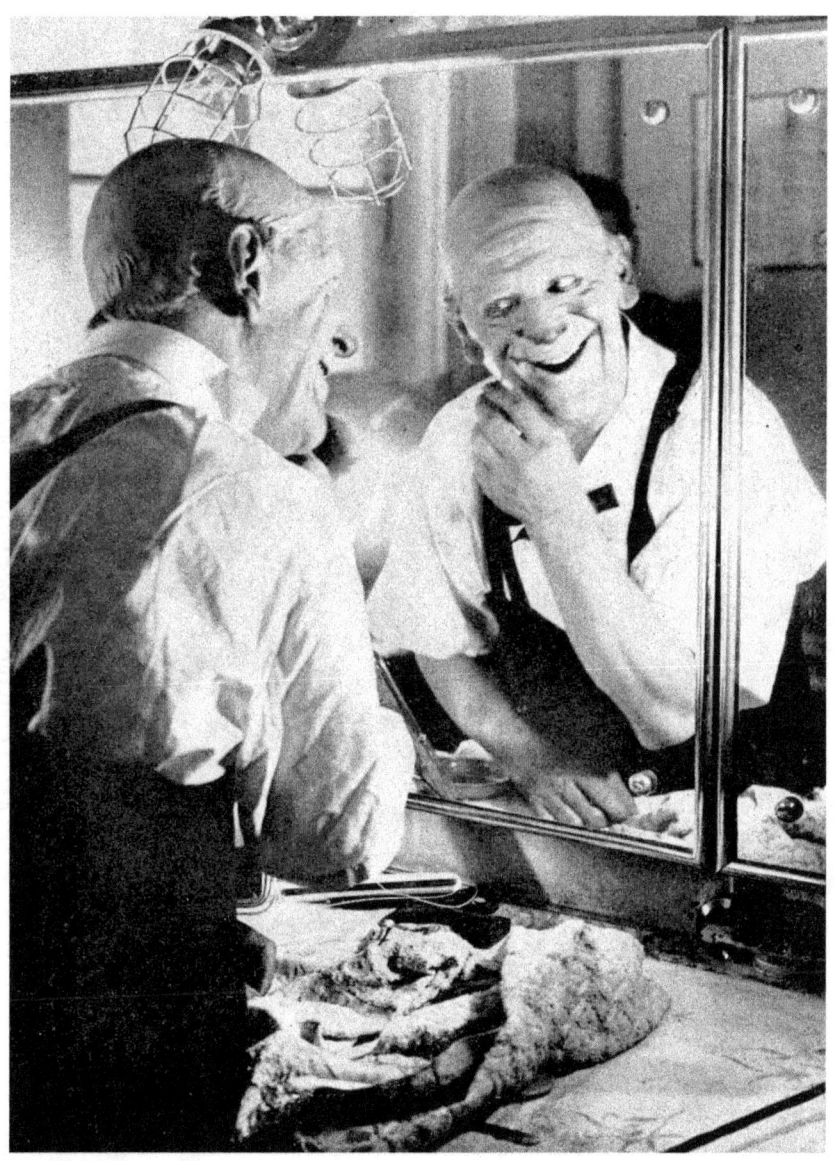

82 Grock

83 The Dratsas plan more Mischief

(harlequinade) poker. He was a sufferer from asthma, had become very corpulent and easily tired. Many a time I have had to assist him out of his wagon and up the ramp, and invariably he swore he would 'never come back to this damned place,' because, so he said, 'the infernal noise hurts my chest.'

In 1933 he grumbled as usual and told me it was the last time I would see him in this 'hullabaloo.' I replied, 'That is an old tale.' 'I mean it this time, and I won't be here next year, *you see*,' he retaliated. He died just before the opening of the 1934 season. There is pathos still surrounding the clowns, however inconsequential their antics may appear to-day. Most of them are 'fill-ins,' appearing from all sides, like an army of vagabonds, between acts. They are merely foils to distract the attention of the audience from the preparations for the next number, and they are expected to invent their own 'gags.' These are often as old as antiquity, not infrequently exciting derision. How many times have they extracted that monstrous tooth from their howling colleague? How many times have those dozen waistcoats been taken off one by one, exposing a ragged but *spotlessly clean* white shirt to view? When old Whimmy Walker chased the youngsters with his red-hot poker he was but repeating an antic of Joe Grimaldi's. It was *expected of him*, and here lies our apology for the clowns of to-day.

Show your own children something funny in the way of a trick and they will give you no peace until you have repeated it over and over again. 'Do it again, Daddy,' is a familiar, and, I'll wager, a universal request.

The clowns know this, and are not very much concerned about your boredom with their ancient jests. It is the simple, the beautiful, or the comical in the circus the children find appealing, and the clowns are loved by them above all.

At any rate a circus without them is unthinkable.

. . . .

The clown and auguste, however, is not always a stop-gap or an 'extra.' He is sometimes the most outstanding personality in the ring. I cannot imagine Sanger's without a

Pimpo and a Pimpo as good as James Freeman at that. To me, who have known him since boyhood, he is the cleverest auguste on earth.

Half a century ago, when older readers thrilled at the coming to town of Lord George Sanger's great circus and menagerie —that one great delight of Victorian youth—'Pimpo' was as clever and as well beloved. But it was not the same 'Pimpo.' It was James the First. The present Pimpo is James the Second, son of the other. He was born in a caravan in the Agricultural Hall, Islington, his natal cry drowned by a tornado of applause from the adjacent matinée crowd. The mighty Blondin, genius of the tight-rope, was 'doing his stuff' round the corner.

Nevertheless, it was a grand entry for Pimpo the Second, and for forty-five years that more or less tumultuous sound has penetrated his ears in recognition of his own accomplishments on the tight-rope, the trapeze, and the high stilts, and as an amazing acrobat, equestrian and juggler.

There is nothing in the entire artistry of the circus that Pimpo cannot do, and do extraordinarily well. His trainers were his own father and his uncle, and, doubtless, certain members of the celebrated Hanneford family, for he toured with that famous show for a period. His life, as a whole, however, has been linked with the destinies of the most celebrated of British circus families, the Sangers, of which family he is a member by marriage. His wife, Victoria, is the daughter of George, the second son of the late Lord John.

Pimpo, when I first knew him, could throw a spring somersault over the backs of nine men and collect his silk hat *en route*. No one else ever performed this prodigious trick, which was as much the speciality of Pimpo as the triple aerial somersault was of Alfred Codona. To-day his nine is reduced to seven, for some time ago he injured the *tendon Achilles*, which is indeed the vulnerable spot of all athletes to-day as it was in Trojan war times. That he can still negotiate the seven bent backs with nothing but a preliminary run, restricted at that by stage limitations, is nothing short of marvellous.

Behind the scenes Pimpo is as comical as he is in front— unconsciously so. The idea of trying to act the clown or speak

84 Pimpo   85 Doodles

86 The Jacksons: Father and Son, but Twins in Art

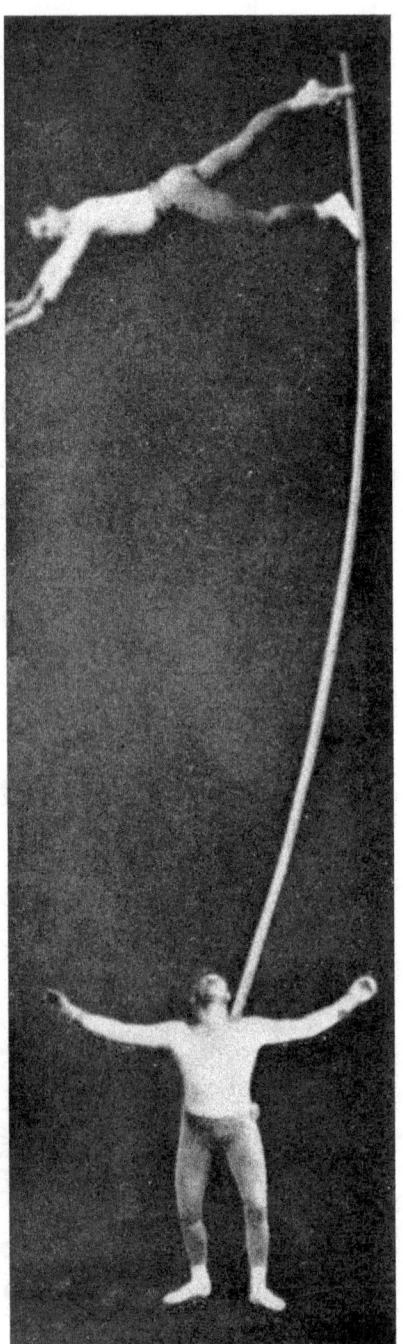

87, 88 Equilibrists and Perchists

with his squeaky voice never occurs to him. You will find him in all the glory of grease-paint mending shoes or making dancing clogs—the elongated 'little Tich' type—or else cooking cutlets for his performing dogs. His dressing-room is a cross between an antiquarian wardrobe and a cobbler's shop. Making his own properties is almost a passion with him.

More diminutive and of a distinctly opposite type is William McAllister, for eighteen years the principal auguste at Hengler's in Glasgow and for as many again at the Blackpool Tower circus. During one season at Olympia 'Doodles,' as he is called, was the highest-paid auguste in Britain. His introduction to circus life was as a wire-walker and high-diver (into the net) at twelve years of age. He travelled the world for twenty years, excelling in feats of dare-devilry, and then became a clown 'by accident.'

His own account of the change is not without humour:

'I was at a summer circus at Scarborough in which I had nothing much to do, and I got fed up and asked the boss if he would let me go with the clowns into the ring. That is how I became a clown. It was at Scarborough where I was clowning that I had my accident. We were playing a water pantomime, and I was a policeman. There was a bridge over the water, and one day, in the excitement, I fell off the narrow bridge into the water, which was in a big tarpaulin, and fractured my collar-bone and was off eight weeks. And yet I dived eighty-four feet into a net time after time without an accident.'

Wherever Doodles appeared children went mad with delight. He could (and can yet) raise shrieks of laughter by a mere gesture. There are few old-timers in circus who will not tell you that for nearly forty years Doodles was the neatest, cleanest and wittiest auguste in the world. His wife is of singular charm and devoted to him. They have two daughters, both clever dancers.

The Yelding family—their name is legion—have produced a crop of talented clowns. Perhaps the most brilliant of them, Harry, decided some years ago to reduce the number of

Yeldings. He and his family, his brother Jack, and his two very pretty sisters Dolly and Milly, all call themselves Sloan. They are all clowns, the two girls included, but clowns *plus*. Harry is the champion stilt-walker of the world, and every member of the group excels in stilt-walking, or some other form of artistry. They are all extremely ingenious and can always be relied upon to stage an act of their own. Harry Sloan has been with the Bertram Mills' show for many years. He is a peculiar mixture of the cynic and the optimist. In lugubrious mood, everything can be of the most dramatic moment to Harry, but the most dramatic moment, one which might have altered every circumstance of his life, occurred when he was not present.

Mrs. Sloan was nursing her baby in the living-wagon about eighteen months ago. It was a warm summer evening and the caravan door was open. She was not aware that three of Togare's Bengal tigers had escaped until one of them thrust his white-ruffed head into the doorway. Mrs. Sloan sat clutching her baby, unable to move with terror. This saved her, for the tiger dived below the wagon and roared. The nets were brought up and the animal captured.

A former champion stilt-walking clown was Costello, who died two or three years ago. In 1932 we were both guests at the 157th birthday party of Zaro Agha, the antediluvian Turk, who fought against Napoleon. The party was held in the Mills' circus ring, and I shall never forget Costello's pathetic appeal when he saw the ring-fences: 'For God's sake don't take me in there or I shall have to do something.'

One cannot get 'circus' out of the blood or the bones.

The celebrated Grock (Adrian Wettach) I never knew—he deserted the circus for the halls. He is, however, of the circus, and I know many of his personal friends. Among these are Theodore Delfin and Charley Mayer, who worked with Grock before he became the partner of Antonnet. Theodore (clown) and Charley (auguste) are both French, both musicians, and both extremely funny. Theodore loves pretty costumes and wears tunic-breeches of three different colours, each of which consists of 46,000 spangles sewn together separately. There is not a great circus in the world in which these two have not appeared. Theodore's radium-painted tunic, the first ever worn by a clown, is a beautiful and ingenious creation.

I cannot mention you all at length, you comrades of mine in motley, rags and extravagant splendour, so I salute, by name only, you of the old time, Joe Craston; you Percy Huxter and Jimmy Mack; Bob Beasy and Tony Gerbola; Little Leslie and Fiery Jack; dear old Pinocchio and all you Austins; Coco (who knows how to get new cars for old), and tiny 'Speedy,' who will run anywhere except from trouble! You are all good fellows and great companions, and because you enrich the world with laughter you are great men.

VII
ACROBATS, JUGGLERS AND WIRE-DANCERS

To lie upon one's back, raise both feet upward and make use of them as a juggler does with his hands is called a 'Risley Act.' A man named Risley introduced this form of acrobatics into the circus round about the year 1868. Several centuries ago scores of tumblers were doing it all over Europe. They can be seen in the miniatures of many illuminated MSS.

Risley acrobats are amazingly clever. They juggle with and throw the human body as easily and with as much accuracy as they do a barrel. Usually they are spring-board artistes as well, varying their act with flip-flaps and somersaults. The group consists of anything from six to nine, one of them as a rule being a lady. The Asgards' speciality is a spring somersault to the shoulders of the third mounter, making the top mounter the fourth man high. This is now featured by the Italian Frilli group, one of the cleverest spring-board acts in the world. One of their tricks is akin to the miraculous. A peculiarly-shaped chair mounted upon a perch is placed at some distance from the spring-board. The catcher sits in the chair and waits for the somersaulting partner to be thrown. When the acrobat is hurled from the spring-board, with some velocity, he describes a double somersault during his passage. The catcher, timing perfectly the journey, throws himself backward in the chair and *catches his partner on one foot*. I have seen this trick some dozen times and do not remember one failure. The Allisons, the Alfredos, the 'Magyars' and the Maschinos are among the best of circus acrobats to-day.

Low-wire acts can be every bit as clever and even more entertaining than the sensational high-wire acts. Were a vote taken among circus artistes themselves as to the cleverest and most graceful performer of the present day I believe the name of Con Colleano would head the poll. Colleano is an Australian

89 Chinese Contortionists

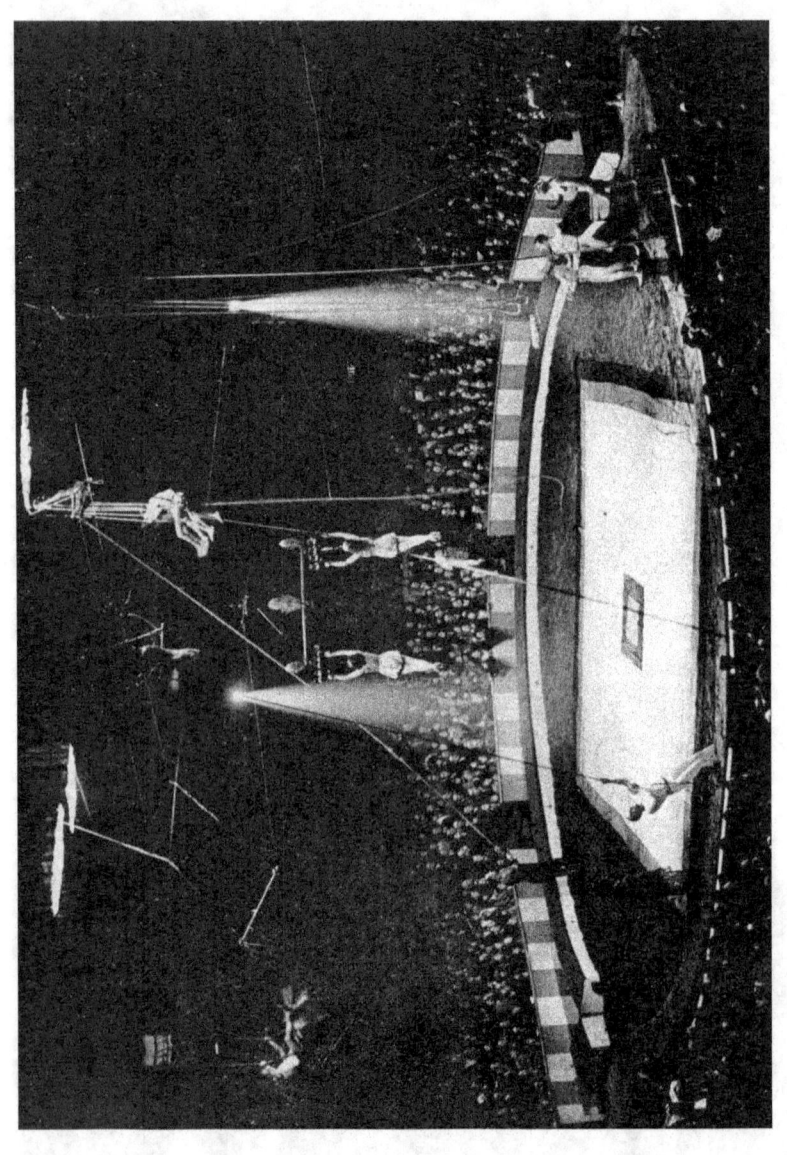

90 Human Butterflies: the Balzer Sisters play the Bells while suspended by the Teeth-grip

91 Exotics: the Hadji Ali Arab Tumblers

92, 93 Con Colleano. He dances a Tango on the Taut Wire, turns a Somersault, and strips off his costume during it

of Spanish extraction and was brought up in the circus. For sheer artistry there is not his equal in the world. From the moment he enters the ring in matador costume his personality gets the audience. Before mounting the wire he 'plays' an imaginary bull with his red-lined cape, making all the favourite passes, including the 'Veronica,' while executing a graceful dance. On the wire itself this incomparable artiste performs tangos, jotas and fandangos with a beauty of movement and balance marvellous to behold. During one dance he turns a somersault, stripping his loose trousers off while turning, and landing upon the wire in silver knee-breeches. His *finale* is a double forward somersault on the wire. He is the only man who has accomplished this trick. His sisters and brothers are all circus stars, one sister, an aerialist, being one of the few trapeze artistes who can catch the bar, and swing from it, by the heel.

This is done by Fritzi Bartoni, who, like Tamara, works solo and staggers many an audience with her daring. Low-wire acts, like the low-trapeze acts, are usually enlivened by some clowning. The clown is either an auguste or a charlie, and is more than likely the cleverest member of the troupe. Fratellini and Rivels both affect the Chaplin costume but their antics are sometimes overdone and a little cutting would improve their acts by 100 per cent.

The Wolkens, on the other hand, do not labour the comedy element, which is extremely funny. The auguste tumbles from poles, ladders and trapeze-bars, landing upon the sawdust in the most grotesque falls time after time, yet every time he rises he gravely searches in his pocket and *brings out a glass of beer*. It is a very clever bit of fooling, and the more puzzling to the audience when he raises the glass to his lips and drinks the contents. The glasses may be trick ones, but there is still the mystery of their secretion in his frowsy garments.

Now let us glance up to the dome sixty feet above and watch Cubanos, the 'Flying Dutchman.' His act is the most bloodcurdling thing in the circus. It is unbelievably daring. Up an apparently never-ending and perilously swaying rope-ladder this slim half-nude figure climbs to a rope suspended 'clothesline' fashion from a steel bar. Upon this rope, which hangs in a broad loop, Cubanos sits astride, and after various terrifying evolutions begins to swing from side to side until a most alarming speed is reached. His hands, meanwhile, see-saw in the air, clap against his thighs or clasp the back of his head. His body maintains a perfect equilibrium while the swinging rope describes its arc. This performance, weird in itself but made more so by the spot-light playing upon the white figure in the dark dome, is thrilling enough in all conscience, but Cubanos has a *bonne bouche* for his anxious watchers.

He leaves his rope and climbs higher still, reaching a wooden platform near the roof. Some thirty feet distant from the platform hangs a trapeze, and we hold our breath while the ringmaster announces, 'Cubanos will attempt to leap from his spring-board to the trapeze—a distance of thirty feet.' There is no net between him and the hard surface of the ring seventy feet below. The small white figure raises his arms like a diver, makes a preliminary crouch and launches his body through the air. He reaches the trapeze, but horror of horrors, the impact is too much for the slender bar. The entire apparatus collapses, and as his body falls every member of the audience jumps to his or her feet in horror. Unknown to the spectators Cubanos is hobbled by the ankle and before reaching the limit of his fall he jerks his body upward and seizes the rope with his hands. This is a more dramatic variation of the trick performed by the lady of the Vesses' troupe. Within the last seven years two men have lost their lives in attempting it.

Cubanos sat on the ring-fence one morning earnestly watching the writer having a little trouble in a cage of lions. On coming out he shook his head sadly and said in quaint English, 'Every man to his taste; come upstairs and I'll teach you my rope trick.' 'I may be a trifle daft,' I replied, 'but I'm not mad!'

Bombayo, a small, handsome and intelligent young Hindoo, has perfected a rope act of great originality. A fairly thick rope with powerful rubber terminals is stretched between two uprights. Upon this 'bouncing' medium he performs a series of gymnastic exercises finishing with a double somersault and landing upon his feet. Bombayo is a splendid showman and 'sells' his act well. He travels with his pretty wife and

94 The most difficult Feat of All. Con Colleano's *Forward Somersault on the Wire*

95 The Human Pyramid

96 The Change-over: The Allisons' 'Risley' Troupe

97 The De Luca Sisters: Strong-Girl Hand-Balancers

98 The comical 'Gold-Dust Twins'

99 Trixie is only sixteen—but *Rastelli* trained her

two-years-old child 'Charlie.' Charlie is the most delightful and lovable little morsel of chocolate-coloured trouble on tour. During the tenting season of the Bertram Mills' show that child bore a charmed life. He wandered from the parental care with clockwork regularity, and was so tiny that it was not easy to find him. Not once only was he found grooming the elephants with a brush, or playing in the stalls of the stallions. That infant was calculated to cause more nerve wrecks than the most hair-raising act in the circus.

Equilibrists who perform upon cycles are plentiful to-day and always popular when they bring along something new. The Paetzolds are shriekingly funny, but Maysy and Brach are astounding. The male member carries his partner on his shoulders while pedalling a single wheel from a seat perched six feet above it. This trick must have taken years upon years to perfect. By 'perfect' I mean not only doing a thing successfully but doing it satisfactorily. Some very clever performers and very talented artists make poor showmen. In circus language, they do not 'sell' their acts well. Indifferent artists are sometimes such superb showmen that they can carry off a sheer bluff with amazing success. Circus acts, indeed, fall into these two categories. One group of performers are sensationally clever and their acts enthral because of their intrinsic merit. The other group do nothing extraordinary, but 'sell' their stuff in an extraordinary way.

You may hold your breath to the point of discomfort at the aerial gyrations of the Balzer sisters, but you hold your sides in the sweet agony of laughter at the capers of the Gold Dust Twins. Nothing funnier ever appeared in a circus ring—yet all that these coloured clowns do is stage a boxing match in which the Queensberry Rules, and all other rules, are broken in the most ludicrous way. Here the thing done is of no account, but the manner of doing it is everything. In your sober moments you will wonder why you laughed, and while wondering you will laugh all over again.

To the outside public the circus world is one of fun, brightness and laughter. To those of us who know it from the inside it is one of hard work, steadfast loyalty and consummate art. The supreme virtue of all circus stars is patience. They not only try and try, but wait and wait, and so conscientious are they that nothing but their best is ever given to the public. Sometimes an artist is assisted by nature—physical beauty is always an asset in the ring, but, as in the case of dwarfs, physical imperfection is exploited with some success.

Contortionists are received, I have noticed, with mixed feelings. Some people are apprehensive of their twisting, doublings and bendings—they do not like to watch such obviously unnatural posturings. Fortunately, most contortionists (it is a very old form of entertainment) are talented in other directions. The Chinese Lai Foun troupe of apparently jointless or boneless young persons are wonderful jugglers, plate-spinners and dancers. This is one of the most graceful of circus acts, made more so by the pleasing beauty of the girls and the charm of the male members.

There are many Chinese tumblers and Risley acrobats who introduce novelties that have little to do with the act proper but insure against boredom. They are particularly fertile in ideas, bizarre in appearance and love colour and brightness. The 'atmosphere' created by a group of exotics is always a happy one. So, too, is that of the cowboy or gaucho act—until the knife-throwing exhibition begins. Then lady members of the audience (and not a few men) grow apprehensive, and sigh with evident relief when the rope-spinning takes its place. The Frank Jackson troupe, the Carsons, and the Dal Paos troupe are the smartest we have seen here since the days of Buffalo Bill's Wild West Show. Even in an act such as this novelties must be worked in for the sake of freshness. So one of the Carsons hurls his knives around the young lady while blindfolded, and one of the Dal Paos boys lassos a galloping horse while standing upon his head. The rope-spinning, like the plate-spinning of the Chinese, is comparatively easy—far easier than the manipulation of the stockman's whips. These necessitate strong wrists and powerful muscles, whilst almost anyone can acquire the knack of spinning a rope and jumping through it.

Whenever I watch a good juggler my mind wanders back to medieval times and I think of the beautiful legend of the jongleur of Notre Dame and the modernised version so

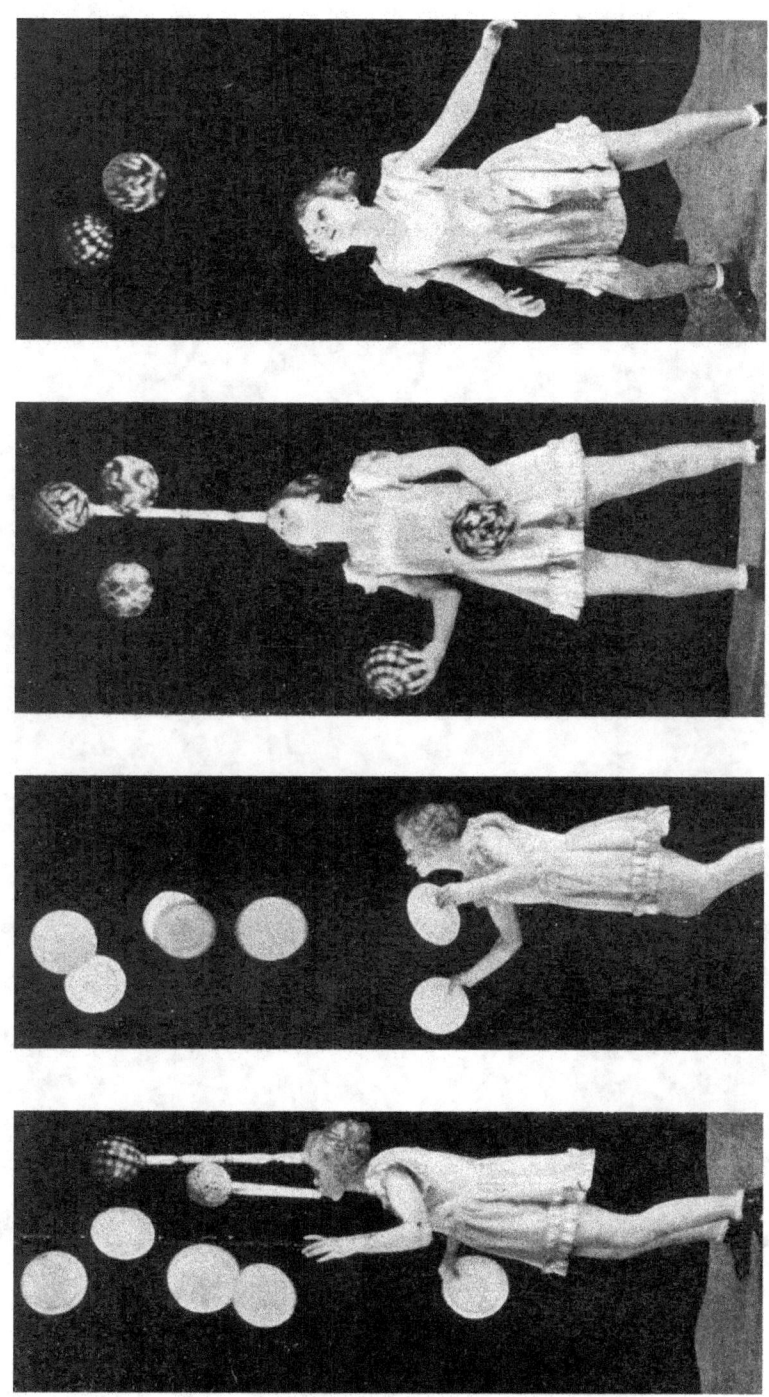

100, 101, 102, 103 Trixie: Four Studies of this amazing Child Juggler

104, 105 Balancing Feats Extraordinary: Maysy and Brach are the World's cleverest Cycle-equilibrists

exquisitely done by Anatole France. There were possibly more jugglers in the Middle Ages than in International Circus. I believe juggling began in the early Stone Age, growing naturally from the dexterity acquired in hurling artifacts at wild animals. Jugglers of necessity are ambidextrous, but the majority of mankind are not—and Professor Elliott Smith assures us they were not so in paleolithic times. Yet many savages, the primitive men of to-day, are ambidextrous. Our 'right-handedness' is largely a matter of accident. Early humans found they could do most things better by using one hand as a tool and the other as a vice. That the right hand became the 'tool' was purely accidental. This may be moonshine, for the real solution will have to be sought for in the brain, not in the hand.

What extraordinary people jugglers are! 'Madame Asra allows a billiard ball to hit the trigger of a pistol which is fixed on her forehead and is fired by the impact.' A little girl, Trixie, performed in London's Olympia last year and caught every ball thrown at her by members of the audience. Not much in that, says the reader, but Trixie caught these balls on a wooden pin held in her mouth. She kept them there too. If the ball bounced but two inches from the ring Trixie threw herself at full length and always got her pin below it—lifting it and keeping it balanced until the applause subsided. This child was fifteen years old. Practice certainly makes perfect, but juggling is a gift. We do not get the chance to see the Asras, the great Rastelli, Salerno or the Perezoffs, and alas! the one and only Cinquevalli is dead. We can watch with delight the exquisitely tasteful and brilliantly clever act of the Carlton sisters who hurl clubs at one another with such rapidity and amid flickering light, that the air seems to be alive with dancing clubs. I have not heard of the boy juggler, Jean Florian, since he appeared at Gordon Bostock's circus, Earl's Court, seven or eight years ago, but he ought to be a top-liner to-day.

Yes! these are all good circus folk, but their prototypes flourished (let us hope) on village common and in baronial hall centuries ago. That was when the Roman circus was not even a memory and the modern circus was undreamt of.

One has to smile when told that such and such an act is not 'circus.' What is 'circus'? Nothing but an equestrian display? It began with that, but it grew, and a circus performance to-day without pre-circus contortionists, ropedancers, tumblers, jongleurs and acrobats would not be a circus at all.

When Mr. Bertram Mills staged the beautiful and spectacular Golden Statuary tableaux at Olympia in 1933-4, many wiseacres shook their heads and said, 'Very pretty, but it is not "circus"!' They forgot that Ducrow introduced the *poses plastiques* at Astley's at least a century ago, the mere fact that his studies of classical statuary were made on *horseback* making no difference whatever.

Astley's hired their first elephant from Cross's Exeter Change Menagerie in 1828. Four years later a lion, tigress and their hybrid cubs were exhibited there by Ducrow and West, who hired them from Atkins, the travelling showman. In the ring that year four zebras appeared. No performance took place with any of these animals—no one thought such performances possible. To-day they take place in every large circus, but again, there are people who regard the introduction of any animal, other than purely domestic ones, into the ring as not 'real circus.'

A trained elephant or zebra act is as much a true circus act as the exhibition of trained horses.

I have tried to show how the circus gradually absorbed the vagabond performers of olden days, giving them the status of a profession. They are no longer 'mountebanks at a fair,' but artistes—many of them of culture and refinement. I shall now endeavour to trace the origin and development of wild animal acts and to show how they were inevitably destined to become 'circus.'

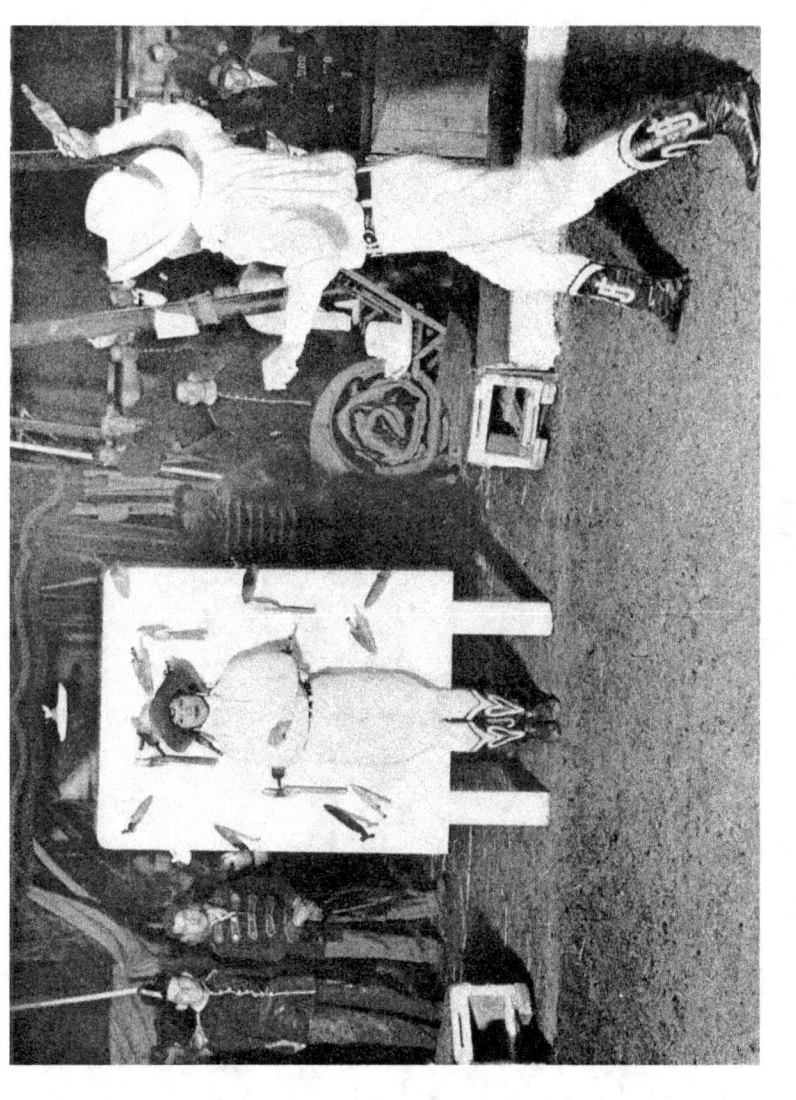
106 The Human Target. Frank Jackson hurls Tomahawks and Knives at his Sister—but they always miss her

107 A Symphony in Black and Gold. When Ears lie Flat and Gums are Bared—*Beware!*

VIII

MAN AND BEAST

IN his delightful foreword to *Widecombe Fair* my old friend, Eden Phillpotts, elaborates the creed of the humanist, and argues that art—literature, painting, sculpture—human character and life itself will be enriched 'when our intellect shall gauge the brain of the tiger and penetrate the bark of a tree, so that the artist may look out of the brute's eyes and from the tree's leaves, not with human values but with measures animal or arboreal.'

When this becomes an achievement, as it might well a thousand years hence, the lost golden age dreamed of by poets and seers will surely dawn. Tennyson's world without discord will become a reality, and man will have power over the animal kingdom.

Power or dominion over others he has in plenty, but it is not the enduring power of kinship or love. Bridle, bit, spur and goad, lash and spear and large-calibre rifle, gin and snare and pitfall confer power—the power of the bully which increases hatred. The triumph of conquest over crude brute force without such doubtful aids is experienced by few, and it is the most thrilling and beautiful thing in life, for it is born of love and of the Psyche.

The human mind has evolved through countless ages, in each of which fear and distrust of animate nature had been inculcated. If we can blame the impersonal, then Nature is at fault, for struggle bred savagery, its resultant carnage bred fear of pain and fear breeds hatred. Man, however, since his conquest of the natural environment, still fears and still hates. This defect is only partly inherited from his prehistoric past; much of it is due to false education. This has raised a barrier, a formidable one at that, between him and his lowlier relatives, and until that barrier is removed the animal will, in turn, fear and hate man. I am afraid the 'little child shall lead them' days are a long way off.

In the conquest of the natural environment man necessarily divorced himself from the rest of his fellow-animals. They remained in a state of nature; he became artificial. He brought one animal along with him—the wolf, which he transformed into a dog. As man lost touch with nature so did the dog. That is why the man is not merely the dog's master, he is his very god. Of no other domestic animal, not even the horse, can this be said. Man is lonely, and he has made this one animal as lonely as himself. It is dependent upon him, not for food alone, but for *sympathy*. There is an *affection* between man and dog, and the wonder of it is that the dog seeks it always, the man only at times.

Between man and every other creature, wild and domestic, there is an element of distrust and in some cases absolute fear. Lions and tigers will kill him, horses have to be 'mastered' and 'broken,' cats will forsake him for their old haunts or the wild, even the parrot will attack him, and the canary fly away. Only the dog sticks by him with a fidelity unparalleled in the world.

If man in the mass fears animals, it is equally true that animals fear man. They do not fear him, however, in lands where man has not persecuted them. They actually become friendly or at least non-hostile. The Kruger National Park, where the lions walk up to the automobiles in spite of the man scent, and the American animal sanctuaries or reservations where the bears do precisely the same thing, prove this. Arctic explorers have told us of the difficulties experienced in unloading supplies because of the congregation of inquisitive penguins. So little fear of man had they, in these regions where man had never been, that they had to be driven away.

This at least inspires a hope, however forlorn, that 'nature's social union,' as Burns called it, so ruthlessly broken by man, may be re-welded.

There are remote fastnesses in jungle and forest populated by primitive folk who have never sundered the subtle bond of kinship between man and his alleged inferiors. In some parts of Africa, Malaya and South America there are native tribes living at peace with the animal kingdom. A mutual confidence has been established on the live-and-let-live principle.

When the great traveller, Humboldt, journeyed through South America he reached an Indian village on one of the reaches of the Orinoco. He was the first white man there and he found the so-called savages mild and generous in disposition. There were no tom-toms banging, no tomahawks threatening and no whoops of defiance. The Indians calmly collected round the white men and nearly every one was accompanied by a monkey which nestled upon his breast.

'They hugged these monkeys like children,' wrote Humboldt.

He described the funny little black-faced, curly-tailed *barrigudo* unknown to Europeans at that time, and ever since then that lovable and delightful creature has been known as Humboldt's Woolly Monkey.

In distant Peru there is another tribe of very primitive Indian people called the Campas. They were written about learnedly by Ordinaire in *The Ethnological Review* (1887). They are peaceful and tolerant people, with a profound respect for tribal custom and ordered life. The article contains a remarkable paragraph:

'They possess a great number of tamed animals, paroquets, ourax, monkeys of several species, ronsocos (capybaras) and even wild boars and tapirs, and it is curious to see the mistress of the lodge (village) when she goes to draw water from the river. If their presence around the habitation attracts at times the puma and tigrillo, they destroy great numbers of insects and small vermin, definitely more dangerous to man than the mountain animals. Their devotion to their masters is the more solid because *it is voluntary and nothing prevents their regaining their liberty*.

'The Campas do not eat the animals thus domesticated; on the contrary, it is not rare to see a savage woman give her breast in turn to her child and to a young monkey.'

Some years ago, visitors to a remote farm in Western Canada were surprised to see a full-grown puma romping with the collie-dog in a field adjacent to the steading. The puma had been captured as a cub and had grown up to become part of the farm livestock. The recent very beautiful film story about the stag and the puma (*Sequoia*) was not at all 'far-fetched.' Domestication seems to have become a lost art—lost since prehistoric times. That man could succeed in taming more than he has done so far, such instances as the above at least indicate.

Humboldt was amazed at the monkey episode on the Orinoco, but these Indians were equally astounded when they saw the white man's pussy-cat. They knew only the killers—puma, jaguar, ocelot—and they could not understand such a phenomenon as a tame killer, for the cat is Nature's supreme slaughterer.

What about the caged wild animals? the reader will ask. Can man become on terms of friendship with such captives? Is it not the height of cruelty to pen a wild animal behind bars? Is it not monstrous to compel such captives to perform tricks which are unnatural? All these questions have to be faced and answered; therefore it is essential that the reader should know and appreciate the precise difference between men and animals. Psychologists limit the definition of 'think' to certain elaborate processes of the human mind. An animal, therefore, does not *think*, for thinking actually means reasoning. A human being can not only think, but think abstractly. No animal on earth can do that. Man is enabled to do it because he is not entirely natural, but largely artificial. He thinks in words, and the words are part of a vocabulary belonging to a language which human society has been creating for thousands of years.

It is this language—the result of articulate human speech—which gives him an intellect, and no animal but man has an intellect. That is why no animal ever wrote a poem or a drama, painted a landscape or invented a machine. These feats are not done by instinct—they are the products of a genius which would be useless without that purely artificial thing called education.

Education, by means of which a portion of the accumulated knowledge of the race is transferred to each individual after it reaches a certain age, is a social product also. Surely this fact—the fact of intellect—is self-evident and needs no prolonged stressing. It marks man from savagery to civilisation, as an abnormal creature. No animal on earth or that ever was on earth is anything like him—except in form, for there is not much difference between him and any of the anthropoid apes. It is the possession of the intellect which makes the difference, and intellect is the product of human society which evolved a language.

In short, all men are animals with an animal inheritance, but no animal (save man) has risen to the human stage. Animals' minds work with images, not with words or ideas. They infer *perceptually*, while man infers *conceptually*.

A monkey can use a lever, but a man understands *the principle of the lever*. A gorilla band will sit round a glowing camp-fire left by hunters, but they have not the (human) sense to add fuel to it.

There are no rigidly hard and fast lines separating all animal acts from all human acts, but the difference is tremendous. No animal's behaviour is controlled by moral principles. Generally speaking, they do not rise from behaviour to conduct. This is not to say that some, indeed many, animals are not loyal, affectionate, kindly and unselfish, but to emphasise that man alone conducts himself or controls his actions in reference to an ideal. The argument is not less sound because certain men are worse than any wild beasts in their conduct towards their fellows.

Now no man is free, that is, wholly free, nor is the animal in the wild free. Hunger, thirst, enemies, disease—all these hedge the wild creature in and make it a bundle of nerves. Under captivity it loses its apprehension of terror. It gains confidence and becomes less suspicious. That is, when taken early in life.

These characteristic changes are easily observable. We say the animal has become 'tamer.' It would not become tamer, but infinitely more savage or intractable if captivity made it unhappy.

This is all very plausible, say the Axel Munthes and other critics, but put it to the test by opening the cages and giving the animals the choice. They do not appear to know that this has been done over and over again. The present writer has done it with jackdaws, sparrows, badgers and foxes. Did they fly or run away to the wild woods? They did not. They had to be chased out of the kitchen which they entered whenever they got the chance. I once owned a corncrake which hunted in the field by day and perched under my chair at night.

Animals in captivity can be made unhappy by cruel people, but captivity of itself does not worry the animal one bit. The caged lion or tiger may excite pity in extremely sentimental people, but they ought to know that the cage is 'home' to the lion. He was probably born in a cage, reared in a cage, and neither knows nor can know of any other world than a world of cages. And life in a cage is not cruel unless evil men make it so.

It is extremely difficult to get animals to leave their cages, as everyone with experience knows. That great world of so-called freedom—the forest, the jungle or the Arctic waste—is a pitilessly cruel place. A realm of hunters and hunted, of massacre, pain, hunger and horrific fear. The caged animal escapes all this, and because it loses fear of the wild, and eventually fear of man, it becomes tamer, and will permit liberties no wild animal outside would tolerate.

An animal has few wants beyond food, sex-satisfaction and safety. It does not hanker after free libraries, income-tax rebates or indulge in political, religious or philosophical speculation. So long as it eats well, rests contentedly and breeds in its captivity, we know it is 'happy'—and most of them do just that.

It is not 'natural' to keep creatures locked behind bars, but it is far better to keep a tiger there than let it add to the 25,000 yearly human deaths from tigers, bears and snakes in India that have not been 'robbed of their freedom.'

It is not 'natural' for men to fly to Australia, read newspapers, smoke cigars, or eat fire-cooked food.

Why should a lion in a cage always excite such pity? When the fine lion Cecil was given its freedom at Whipsnade it began to decline. The Zoo officials were compelled to cage it again and send it to Regent's Park, where the caged life and the crowds helped it to recover. This lion was a wild lion caught when a little cub and treated gently by man, and it had always been used to the excitement of menagerie life. Animals do not know that they are in captivity. They do not *reason* like human beings; they do not *feel* like human beings; and they are not gifted with imagination.

Do not project your own mind into the skull of a polar bear, and do not picture yourself as a bear 'robbed' of something it does not really value. I have seen the 'soulful' eyes of a bear when it was engaged in tearing the throat from a dear friend of mine, and that was a trick it had inherited from its polar ancestors who knew not cages. This same bear used to take sugar from our lips and steal from our pockets, but the cruelty bred in it by that shockingly cruel thing called the 'freedom of nature' came uppermost at an inopportune moment.

One more point I ought to emphasise, and that is the question of space. To confine an animal in too small a cage is definitely cruel. But that is quite different from what *man* thinks too small a cage.

A matchbox is a huge palace to a bee, as anyone who peeps into a clustered bee-hive, wasps' or ants' nest will agree. Many animals (lions particularly) are indolent creatures, and lie all day in the one spot under a tree or in a cave. They only move when hunger drives them, and if the prey is near by they do not move more than is necessary.

I repeat, it is an absurd thing to attribute to a captive beast the sufferings, mental anguish, desires and aspirations which a sensitive, intellectual man (the product of an evolutionary revolution and of ten thousand years of social development) would experience under the same circumstances. It is sheer sentimentality gone mad.

I have had far too much experience among captive animals to believe them unhappy (unless made so by brutality or deprivation). The animal's reactions to captivity vary according to type, but in ninety-nine cases out of a hundred they become contented and, therefore, 'happy' when they are well treated and have lost their fear of man.

I have been on friendly terms with all kinds of wild, semi-wild and domesticated animals for over thirty years. Not one of them has injured me other than accidentally. I have been kicked by a horse (because a hen irritated it); I have had my thigh seized by a full-grown lion (because it was in pain); I have been gripped twice by very large tigers and got away unscathed. I have twice faced the angry spring of huge lions (one of which killed a keeper only three months later), and stopped them both with nothing but a voice and a handkerchief, and I have had some weird experiences with the somewhat brainless serpent family, both venomous and constricting kinds. Scores of less important creatures, leopards, wolves, monkeys, apes, hyenas, otters, lynxs, polecats and their relatives, have taken me to their bosoms in brotherly or sisterly love. I have scarcely any scars on my body, and those I have were due entirely to my own folly.

I have been foolish enough to place my head between the jaws of lions and tigers, have hugged, and wrestled with, both these monsters, have taught them to kiss me, and have sat astride them like the Una of mythology. Not once but many times. But let me say that these liberties, so seemingly impossible, cannot be taken with *every* lion, tiger, bear or even elephant. This is where one's knowledge helps. Every animal has its own individual character, like a man. That character—the varying moods, caprices, idiosyncracies—must be studied before risks are taken. Even the creature's state of health must be considered. A tiger will kiss you to-day and kill you to-morrow. A lion will lick your head to-night and bite it off to-morrow night. One never knows, and never fears. Men have been killed in the lions' den because a tin-tack or a wood splinter irritated a beast at the wrong moment. There are no 'tame' lions or tigers and there are no 'safe' rules.

Some people are in less danger than others, and some can compel even affection from the most relentless of carnivores. It is all a question of mutual faith. Wild animals are not automata—they have intelligence if they lack intellect. They *know* things. They know exactly what you are when you approach, and they know what is in your mind. You radiate either fear, hostility or the placidity of confidence, respect and love.

Timidity and distrust provoke their antagonism; sympathy, born of a complete understanding, allays their suspicion and preserves tranquillity. I believe even the body odour of a human being is influenced by his state of mind and in turn influences the animal, but I cannot prove this. Whenever I

108 Cronies: Tshaka and the Author

109 White Killers of the Frozen North

110 The Author hugs a Playmate . . .

111 And Instructs Emir

approach a wild animal I try to do so as one of themselves. They become my equals, for I know I am only their superior in mind. They soon recognise that and are responsive.

Friendship with our fellow-men and women depends so often upon the method of approach, and wisdom comes with experience. It would be a happier world if the loud and hectoring voice were hushed, if we could but always see the other fellow's point of view, or gauge the brain of a tiger and peer at life through the windows of a serpent.

IX
'LION TAMERS' OF OLD

THE wild animal acts of the circus had their origin in the performances which took place in the wagon-cages of the travelling menageries or 'wild-beast shows' of the nineteenth century. There were itinerant menagerists in the eighteenth century, like Pidcock and Polito, whose 'Royal Menagerie,' Exeter Change, stood on the site of the Strand Palace Hotel. In these shows there were no performing animals—they were purely travelling zoos.

Polito and his collection of animals were shipwrecked on a journey to Ireland in the 'thirties of last century. His building in the Strand was taken over by Cross, the enterprising animal dealer. Long before this, however, George Wombwell had appeared upon the scene. This remarkable man was born near Saffron Walden in 1777. A cordwainer by trade, he established a business in Soho, but, at the age of thirty, became a travelling showman. His animal repository was in Commercial Road, and here was stabled the first giraffe ever imported. George, or 'Jerry' as he was called, took to the road in 1805 and was soon the greatest showman in Britain. Twenty-two years later his exhibition of wild animals cleared £1,700 in receipts at Bartholomew Fair, the record for that year. His great rival in the show line was Atkins, who, according to Hone, had a clean, spacious and representative collection of wild animals, including lion-tiger hybrids. Royalty frequently patronised both shows, but Wombwell's outshone the other and grew so extensively that when he died, in 1850, Wombwell had three large menageries on the road. Number one he had managed himself, working in a smock and scrubbing wagons like his meanest workman. Number two was under the direction of Mr. and Mrs. Edmunds (Mrs. Edmunds was his niece), and number three was looked after by his nephew George Wombwell. To the Edmunds' show came the first Bostock as horsekeeper, an important post when we learn that Wombwell

112 The Interior of Wombwell's Menagerie when Fairgrieve owned it

113 Carl Hagenbeck   114 E. H. Bostock

115 Interior of Polito's Menagerie at Exeter 'Change, 1812

had a stud of horses numbering one hundred and twenty—divided between the three concerns. James Bostock became publicity agent, married Emma Wombwell (Mrs. Edmunds' sister), secured two royal commands for the show, and prospered generally. After Wombwell's death he commenced business on his own account, Edmunds' menagerie continuing under the name of Edmunds.

James Bostock was the father of E. H. Bostock who, on growing to manhood, bought out his widowed mother and adopted from her the combination name, 'Bostock & Wombwell.' Meanwhile Edmunds' first show was passed on to Fairgrieve, their second ultimately became part of Bostock & Wombwell's. Besides these well-known shows there were other travelling wild animal exhibitions. Ballard's became popular because of a rather sensational mishap. In 1816 one of their lionesses escaped and attacked the leading horse of the Exeter mail.

There was plenty of advertisement in this for Ballard, and he was still booming his Exeter mail lioness nine years later at Bartholomew Fair. Hilton's travelled for a period but eventually sold out to Mander's, who became the only worthy competitors of Bostock & Wombwell's. Other menageries of less importance were Sedgewick's, Anderton & Rowland Day's (with whom the present writer travelled), Chipperfield's, Braham's, and Kayes'. Many of these were touring just prior to the Great War, and some of them, as mere 'lion shows,' may be seen on the modern fairground.

We need journey no farther back than the nineteenth century to find the first 'Lion Tamer'—that is, the first we have any authentic information about, and the first to be 'billed' as such. He was undoubtedly the man known as 'Manchester Jack,' the lion keeper of Wombwell's menagerie, not the American Van Amburgh who is credited with that distinction. Long before Van Amburgh appeared in this country the public were invited to see 'Manchester Jack' sit on the back of Nero and open the lion's mouth. Nero was an old lion in 1835, but had always been good-tempered. Ten years previously this lion with his fellow exhibit, Wallace, had figured in a celebrated battle with bandogs at Warwick. Nero took no notice of the dogs, but Wallace tore them to shreds. (Wallace and a tigress subsequently escaped from their cages and killed four people).

Van Amburgh came from America with a group of lions, tigers and leopards all trained to perform, and wonderfully trained they were too. He was certainly the first man to perform with a 'mixed' group, among which was a melanic tiger, the first ever seen in this country. At Astley's he was starred in a spectacular scene from Eugene Sué's *Wandering Jew*, entitled 'Morok the Beast Tamer'—the wild-animal act had come to the circus.

Frost says Van Amburgh was engaged by Ducrow and West, but the bill from which I have taken these particulars gives the name of William Batty as proprietor of Astley's. It was under Batty's management in 1842-4 when the next famous 'Lion King,' Carter, performed with a lion, a jaguar, and possibly a tiger, though this is doubtful. Descriptions were not too accurate in those days. Wombwell called a bison a 'bonassus,' and Atkins named an African antelope an 'aurochos.' Carter's 'Brazilian tiger' might be anything. He certainly rode in a chariot drawn by a garlanded lion, and he wrestled with the 'tiger.'

A poet contributed some verses upon Carter in a popular newspaper of 1844, the first stanza reading:

> Into the jungle or the forest deep,
> He plunges boldly, and the whiskered pard
> Or shaggy lion tears from out their lair
> And makes them gentle denizens of towns!

Carter was mauled several times, his hands on one occasion being dreadfully lacerated.

Van Amburgh had introduced a new thrill into public entertainment, and every travelling menagerie and circus now included in the programme a wild-animal act. This performance took place in the wagon; the arena, or big cage, had not been thought of. At the end of the 'forties Hilton's show presented the first 'Lion Queen'; she was Hilton's daughter. Wombwell's (Edmund's), not to be outdone, secured the services of Miss Nellie Chapman, who became the most famous Lion Queen of the day. Then occurred the first cage tragedy. Nellie left Wombwell's in 1849 to become the wife of George Sanger, and a new Lion Queen had to be found. A young woman named Helen Bright succeeded Miss Chapman, but she had neither that young woman's knowledge nor her gentleness. In spite of repeated warnings she persisted in flicking one of the tigers on the face with her whip. At the evening performance at Chatham in January 1850 this tiger sprang upon her, seized her head in his jaws and crushed it with one bite. She died shortly after being removed from the cage. This put an end to the run of Lion Queens—women were barred, but the men remained.

Sanger, who was now happily married to Nellie, had a show of his own, which by 1854 had risen to the dignity of a circus. In 1858 he bought five lions from Jamrach's, the first he ever possessed, and Crockett, one of his musicians, began to train them. Crockett was one of the best of the early lion men, and his performances at Astley's in 1861 excited the admiration of everyone. Frank Buckland, the naturalist, paid him a handsome compliment when he wrote, 'Many of my readers recollect Van Amburgh and his cageful of lions, but I think Mr. Crockett and his magnificent beasts was a far better performance.'[1]

A few days after Buckland's visit these lions escaped, got into the circus and killed a man named Jarvey. Crockett was sent for, and on arrival found two lions tearing up properties on the stage, a lioness sitting in the Royal box with her paws on the parapet, and another lion holding poor Jarvey down 'as a dog sits over a bone.' He was not long in persuading the beasts to re-enter their cages, but Jarvey could not be saved; he had twenty-seven wounds on his body, some of them dreadful to behold.

Cage tragedies now begin to occur with some frequency, so at this point I would like to say something about the methods of the animal trainer. I do not know how Van Amburgh trained his carnivores, but it is quite evident that all the early English trainers knew the correct methods of approach, otherwise they could never have achieved what they did. They were the first men to 'gentle' a wild animal,

[1] *Curiosities of Nat. Hist.*, Vol. 3.

not to tame it, for a lion, tiger, leopard or jaguar cannot be tamed. This requires elaboration.

One hundred years ago ignorant Continental showmen believed it impossible to enter the cage of a lion or tiger without being attacked or killed, unless the animal was first of all terrorised from the outside. Whips, sticks, pitchforks, guns and red-hot iron bars were part of the paraphernalia of every wild-beast act. An incessant din was made by attendants during the performance, which consisted in making the maddened and bewildered animals spring around the cage until the so called 'lion-tamer' seized an opportune moment to dodge outside.

It was a revolting spectacle, disgustingly cruel, very dangerous to the performer, but evidently thrilling to the spectators. Scores of men were torn to pieces by the tortured beasts, but such tragedies were exploited by the proprietors to attract a sadistic public to the show.

Feeble imitations of this kind of exhibition, but without the cruelty, are occasionally attempted to-day, but the utter senselessness of it brings it at once into disfavour. It is a pure fraud, though quite a harmless one, for the 'untameable' lion is trained to be untameable, and only the greenhorn is deceived.

The 'gentling' method of training carnivorous beasts to perform tricks in a cage was introduced on the Continent by the late Carl Hagenbeck. He was observant enough to see that animals were as varied in their natures as men and women. There are bad lions, mad lions, sad lions, happy lions, clever lions and lions who are stupid. Some are lazy and good-natured, others active and treacherous, many are sullen and unreliable, a few quite sanguine and even affectionate.

There are no safe tame lions, tigers, leopards or bears, and only a fool ever believes it. The big cats are fashioned for killing by stealth and with speed. Fangs, claws, muscles and sinews are to a cat what the cortex of the brain is to a thinker—something that goes on working in spite of temperament. A man who plays about with flesh-eating wild beasts is always in danger, however 'tame' they appear to be, for the reflexes of an animal are quite beyond the control of an animal's brain.

In many of the accidents that have taken place the animals

116 Crockett: a Lion Tamer of Last Century

117 The Death of Helen Bright

118 Bostock and Wombwell's on Tour. From an old Painting

119 Bostock and Wombwell's Combination Circus-Menagerie at Stonehaven. From an old Photograph

were 'kindly' ones—in short, they were those quiet enough to permit liberties; but they were ferocious beasts in spite of all, and disaster overtook the too confident trainer.

Take a young lion or tiger some six months old and keep 'handling' him. He will grow up with a 'human' association which becomes *part of his nature*. But that nature is nine-tenths a killing nature, and man to him is no more than a tree is to the jungle relative. *Some day he will want to sharpen his claws on that adjacent man*, not because he is vicious, but because he is ignorant of man's vulnerability.

When he reaches the age of three years he begins his training. Cages and men are nothing to him but part of his 'jungle.' He is not frightened of them, because he has grown up with them. He is, consequently, a much more ticklish customer than the 'forest-bred' animal. 'Forest-bred' sounds more imposing, but the cage-bred beast is ten times more dangerous than one caught in the wilds as a cub and reared by man. To teach him to perform is a great mercy. It gives him a zest of life and breaks the monotony of captivity, besides providing him with health-giving exercise. Furthermore, he *likes* to perform, for he has a 'love of approbation' and is very susceptible to applause—just as a horse, a dog or a man is.

The first thing he must learn is his name. He probably knows it already, for he has been called it from infancy. He is then tried out with certain tricks, some of which he will not attempt.

It is well to mention that only four lions out of every twenty are intelligent enough to train, and it is these intelligent ones I am writing about.

Now arises the question of character. One lion will spring through a hoop and enjoy it, but nothing on earth will persuade another lion to do it. He will let you open his mouth, perhaps, and even let you peer down his throat, but *he won't jump through a hoop*.

Finding these things out takes time and patience, but it pays, for an animal forced to do anything against its inclination would make a rotten exhibition.

Sometimes a lion or tiger (or any other animal) possesses a peculiar characteristic, like a human being who stutters, for instance, and this is immediately exploited by the trainer for show purposes. I know a lion that lifts his forepaws an incredible height from the ground when he walks. He can't walk any other way. He is exactly like the born trotter among ponies. All that was required here was to train him to sit on the first block in the arena and, when his act came, he walked *quite naturally* around the ring to the music of a fox-trot; and the applause was deafening.

All training is not so easy as this, for many lions and sometimes groups have to be trained to perform in combination. The animals are first kept in association cages, with mesh or bars instead of wooden walls between them. They get to know one another, and soon to disregard one another. Fights cannot be avoided, but they do not often occur. Absolutely irreconcilable animals are excluded at once.

Certain tricks or postures having been taught to the individual animals, they have now to be taught to do these in concert. This takes a lot of time and more patience, for not only must the animals be brought to tolerate each other's presence, but they must 'do their stuff' simultaneously if the act is to be effective.

For months the trainer has been instructing them like a teacher with children. His greatest aids have been bribery with tit-bits, and flattery. He carries a pouch or satchel filled with pieces of raw meat, and never fails to encourage his pupils with flattering words. The animals have to learn definite 'cues,' and these are usually words, gestures or whip-cracks. The whip is never used as an instrument of punishment—it is a guide or aid in the big cage even when the animal is flicked with the thong. Anyone who believes that a lion or tiger can be 'hurt' with a carriage whip can believe anything.

The big cats snarl and roar *at one another*; they cannot help it, and so they snarl and spit at the trainer. He encourages them to do so very often, for it means nothing.

They claw and bite one another in play, and when they do it to the trainer as they sometimes do, he goes to the infirmary —he is a pulpy man, not a thick-hided beast.

The finest trainers are Britishers, Germans and Czechs. They have the necessary phlegmatic temperament and the

120 Julius Seeth: He would sit in their midst and be photographed

121 Julius Seeth with a 'mixed' group of Lions, Ponies and Boarhounds

122 The Author with Adolf Cossmy's Nine Lions. The topmost animal is the rare Indian Lion. Below this one (*right*) is Caesar, a 'wicked' animal

requisite patience. In America the wild-animal man is more often than not a 'slanger.' His methods are out of date, often definitely cruel, and his performance unpleasant to watch. I have seen no wild-animal performance that disgusted me so much as that of Clyde Beatty in the film called 'The Big Cage.' It sounded like the battle of Waterloo, so much idiotic gun-firing went on. Not one of the animals had his confidence and not one of them looked happy. One cannot trust a film, of course; it is faked for sensation value, and Mr. Beatty is doubtless a humane man, but he lent himself to bad publicity in 'The Big Cage.'

By the Hagenbeck method the man becomes the 'pal' of his beasts. He wins their confidence, their respect and not infrequently their affection. He does not 'keep his eye on them,' but turns his back on them. He does not shout at them unless a menacing moment crops up. He never strikes them, and he never frustrates their natural inclination to bite and tear with their claws. When they attack him, as they are always liable to do, he holds out a wooden staff or a wooden fork, and they are usually content to vent their cat-like anger on these. Every time they do the right thing he applauds them with 'Bravo,' and gives them a morsel of meat. In time they understand exactly what is required of them, and once the 'association' is formed the performance is assured.

These are all the 'secrets' there are in the training of wild animals. Some men are better than others because their sense of kinship with their animals is greater. Such men will always be more successful than those who fear or distrust their charges, because animals are quick to sense fear or hostility in a human being and equally quick to take advantage.

Accidents cannot be avoided by the very finest and gentlest of trainers, because animals like lions, tigers and leopards have been trained first by nature, and the process of evolution, to react involuntarily when their suspicion is aroused. Anything strange, from an unrecognised movement to a flash of light or a wasp-sting, will be interpreted by them as a menace. A good trainer and performer must never get panicky, but keep perfect control of himself, must be as agile as a boxer, as patient as Job, and possess a soothing, insinuating voice of low pitch. This ingratiating voice was noticeable in all the successful trainers of the early days. Even big John Cooper, one of the most celebrated lion men, possessed a voice of peculiar timbre which helped him to win the confidence of his charges. John was born in 1833 and joined Hilton's menagerie when ten years of age. How he became a performer is one of the most dramatic stories in show annals.

'We had a large ferocious lion in the show, and the beast had a very interesting habit of occasionally attempting to break out of his cage. In consequence of this he was secured by a collar and chain let down through the roof, no one having ever entered his den. One day, when the show was at Leeds, the collar somehow became loose, and the lion, to celebrate the event, set about trying to demolish the sides of the cage to such purpose that everyone became alarmed.'

Cooper was then an 'apprentice' of eleven years. To the horror of every attendant, the boy walked up the steps of the cage, entered the den, picked up the collar and calmly fastened it around the lion's neck. Coming from the cage without hurt he was seized by Hilton and soundly thrashed for this impudence. Later on he was encouraged to do it again. 'I did,' he says, 'and next day I figured on the bills as the youngest lion-tamer in the world, and the whole time I was with the show afterwards I gave a daily performance with that lion.'

Cat-nature is unfathomable; any other intruder would have been attacked and killed. Cooper worked for a long time with Continental circuses, returned to England, appeared at Bostock and Wombwell's, and died at the age of eighty-seven. The only injuries he received during his forty-eight years of training and performing with all kinds of wild animals were sustained through his interference with the beasts when fighting. On one occasion he was attacked when extricating a lion from a painful predicament.

'While I was going through the afternoon performance, one of the seven lions which I was putting through their facings tried to jump over the barrier and got tangled in the iron bars. Immediately all was confusion. The audience screamed with fright, and the lions careered round the cage roaring fearfully. However, I stayed in the cage and, procuring a hammer, bent the bars sufficient to extricate the entangled lion. Whether the others thought I had done them an injury or not I cannot tell, but no sooner was the lion loose than all of them went for me. The next few minutes was a very exciting time. The audience were now too frightened to scream, and many women fainted. It was no doubt a terrible scene while it lasted, but although my clothes were torn to shreds I managed to escape from the cage with only a few scratches here and there.'

John Cooper wore a huge beard and had shaggy eyebrows. He was on very friendly terms with the late King Edward (when Prince of Wales), received gifts from many other monarchs, and died a confirmed bachelor. He was the contemporary of the black trainer who worked for Manders and became famous as Maccomo. Maccomo, and Dellah of Bostock's, both West Indian negroes and not unlike in appearance, were two of the most intrepid men who ever performed with wild animals. Maccomo, like Van Amburgh, Crockett, Carter and Cooper, died naturally, but William Dellah and Thomas McCarthy, who was Maccomo's successor, both died terrible deaths. Dellah went under the name of Sargano. He became a wild-animal trainer in 1867 and, though frequently mauled, lived until 1892. I saw him perform when a small boy in a country town, and remember him not only as the first 'lion-tamer' I ever saw but the first black man I had ever seen in my short life. The following year he was killed at Hednesford.

He entered the cage to perform with two bears and one spotted hyena at a quarter to ten one winter's night. There was some mud upon his boots, and when he turned in the cage after closing the door he slipped and fell.

It is a curious thing, but, unless an animal has been trained to regard a recumbent man as 'normal,' it will lose all respect for him. *Never fall down in a cage of wild animals.*

The Russian bear sprang upon Dellah and seized his side, while the hyena bit him in the head.

The hyena has the most powerful bone-crushing teeth on earth, and poor Dellah was soon helpless. He cried out, but the second bear rushed over and joined in the attack, and the animals dragged him all over the cage.

Mr. Frank Bostock tried in vain to beat the animals off with a cane, but only when the feeding-forks were thrust into the cage could the mangled body be brought out.

It was terribly injured, but Dellah was not only alive but conscious. He died twenty minutes later, very bravely, trying to smile at the doctor who attended him, and saying: 'God bless everybody—let me die like a man.' Mr. E. H. Bostock has told me many a time that Dellah was the greatest of all his trainers.

McCarthy's fate was even worse, though in some measure due to his own folly. He lacked the coolness and nerve of his celebrated predecessor Maccomo, and contracted the habit of fortifying himself with strong drink. This is the worst thing an animal man can do. Any deterioration of character is 'sensed' at once by the animals, more especially by cats and bears, and sooner or later they lose both their confidence in their master and their respect for him. This is what happened to McCarthy. One night his arm was bitten off. He continued to perform, but with evident fear. Some time later, at Bolton, he was bitten on the wrist, but not severely. It ought to have been a warning, but McCarthy continued drinking. On January 3rd 1872 the end came—at Bolton strange to relate. The entire group of lions attacked him *en masse* and literally tore him to pieces. This was, perhaps, the ghastliest tragedy in all British show history.

Here, by the way, is a curious fact about the nature of big cats. When a tiger attacks one in a cage the other tigers look on indifferently—it is not *their* fight. When a lion gets a man down the other lions 'gang up' and help. Tigers are much more agile and cat-like than lions but, to my mind, they are safer to work with.

123 Adolf Cossmy and the Polar Bear. This Animal killed him a few days later

124 Trubka calls his 'Cats' by name and they turn their Faces to him

X

THE MODERNS

The great animal trainers of to-day are nearly all products of the Hagenbeck training school in Germany. For more than fifty years that school, under such able men as the Hagenbeck brothers, Heinrich and Lorenz (sons of the famous Carl), Richard Sawade, the greatest of all tiger trainers, Fritz Schilling and Willy Peters, have turned out scores of able and humane pupils and hundreds of animal groups most excellently trained. Here were trained the first polar bears in the middle of last century—an achievement up till then believed to be impossible. Hagenbecks have exported more animals, trained and untrained, than any firm on earth, and their trainers are performing to-day in the earth's four quarters. Many of them have visited this country with performing groups, one of the most celebrated, Julius Seeth, as early as 1887. That was at the first Olympia Circus, where his act was witnessed by Queen Victoria, the Princess Margaret and Alice, and Prince Arthur of Connaught. The circus had been brought over from the Paris Hippodrome, and with it came Lockhart's elephants. At that date I was but two or three years of age, my knowledge of wild animals being restricted to the wooden ones of a toy Noah's ark. Some thirteen years later Seeth was here with an astounding group of twenty-eight lions, two ponies and two boarhounds, all assembled in one cage. I was his assistant boy for one month.

Herr Julius Seeth was one of the finest men I ever met. He taught me more about the great cats than any other man, and he knew more about them than any living man. Physically he was a perfect specimen of manhood, a six-footer and broad in proportion. He had the heart of the bravest lion in his magnificent group, and the cool head of a well-trained boxer. He was deliberate without being phlegmatic, took the most terrible risks knowing that they were risks, smiled in the face of the deadliest danger, and never raised his voice above his normal tone of conversation. I have known fellow-countrymen of his equally daring, but few who had such a marvellous power of control over both captured and cage-bred lions as he possessed.

From England he went back to the Continent and journeyed practically all over it, meeting misfortunes now and then which made serious inroads upon his pocket, as well as his health. In Paris he was attacked when in the cage with fourteen lions, and had to lie in bed for four months. The surgeons managed to save his leg (which one lion had bitten through) after contemplating its amputation. At Barcelona a lioness sprang at him, and the pair rolled over and over in the ring until Seeth, exerting his last ounce of strength, threw her from him and staggered out with both arms severely bitten and fifteen other wounds which sent him to hospital for another term. Another attack from a lion at Antwerp was not so serious, his hands bearing most of the wounds made by the beast's claws. These kind of accidents cannot be avoided, for the 'safest' of lions or tigers will suddenly go bad and attack the nearest living thing.

Seeth's fame as a wonderful group performer penetrated to Africa, and he received an invitation from the Emperor Menelik to visit Abyssinia.

It was after his return with a group of lions presented to him in admiration by Menelik II that I became acquainted with him. Menelik's subjects knew lions only as the most dangerous animals on earth. They preyed in forest and desert and had lain waste the cities of men. Of all lions, the Abyssinian lion is the handsomest, for there they are darker-maned and invariably develop the dark fringe along the belly.

Menelik had captured some and, when Seeth arrived, invited him to 'tame' one. The animals were lodged in a strong building with an iron gate, and had never seen a white man in their lives. Accompanied by the Emperor and his suite, Seeth looked through the door, asked the attendant to unlock it, and to the amazement of all, calmly walked into the huge den and all round it. He selected four of the lions, had them shuttered off, and, within a week, had trained them sufficiently well to give a modest performance at the court.

On his departure from Addis Ababa, Menelik's capital, the Emperor presented him with an entire group of lions, including those he had trained.

His group consisted of twenty-eight animals, every one of them of handsome appearance. They were fed in the arena fourteen at a time, and fights would have been frequent but for the presence of the master. Mustapha, a huge, tawny-maned brute, hated Menelik, and Vladimir bore a grudge against Hassan, but so long as the quiet voice of Seeth called their names, trouble never got beyond the challenging roar or the spitting snarl.

In every group there is one or more more morose than the rest and usually one more trustworthy than the others. Seeth's Pasha was a yellow fiend, and Sultan a perfect paragon among lions. He weighed nearly 500 pounds and, at a word, jumped to his double pedestal and stood like a statue, while his strong master grasped him around the thighs and carried him across the ring on his shoulders.

The fetching number in Seeth's performance was the grouping of two big lions, two ponies and two boarhounds in a ring, around which sat twenty-five lions. I have seen the lion stretch down and touch noses with the ponies, so very perfectly had both groups been trained.

Seeth carried a short whip with him as an indicator to the animals, but he seldom even cracked it. It is no abuse of words to say that he could read the 'minds' of lions. He could check an incipient fight with a word or two and elude disaster by waving a finger. This control was exercised outside as well as inside the cages, for Seeth was, like all good trainers, seldom absent from his charges for any length of time.

Like Bonavita, who once toured with twenty-seven lions, he would bring his ferocious herd into the arena and, instead of grouping them on pedestals, would persuade them to lie down, and then without whip, stick, or weapon of any kind, would sit in their midst and be photographed. This was all tremendously wonderful to a boy not long from school, and on asking him one day why the lions did not kill him, he smilingly answered, 'They wouldn't kill you either, sonny; lions know who to kill and who not to kill—you know how to talk to them.'

There are homicidal cats just as there are homicidal men, and aberrations will occur among the best-behaved; but, though one cannot prove it, all animals have a sixth sense and seem to know who to molest and who to refrain from hurting.

Seeth had plenty of ill-luck during his career. In his early days, he was shipwrecked and lost all his animals besides his personal belongings. The greatest tragedy, the one that wrote *finis* to his wild-beast days, occurred in Moscow.

After leaving Britain, he ultimately reached Moscow—the Moscow of old, where honesty was almost unknown. Here someone sold his butcher some meat that was nearly putrid, and next morning every one of his twenty-eight beautiful and perfectly trained beasts was found dead—ptomaine poisoning had killed them.

Since Seeth's day men like Carl Haupt, Richard Sawade, Willy Peters, August Molcker, Alfred Schneider, Rudolf Matthies, Alfred Kaden, Carl and Adolf Kossmeyer, Vojtek Trubka and Alfred Court have travelled the world, some of them with more 'cats' than Seeth exhibited. Most of these very excellent men are my personal friends, and kinder men it would be difficult to meet.

Sawade was one of the first men to group lions and tigers together. He is retired now, but for thirty-three years he toured the globe. A man of more indomitable courage and energy it would be difficult to find. There were two occasions at least when Sawade triumphed over death in horrible form by sheer force of courage. In Buenos Aires he was busy opening the cage to permit his six tigers to enter the arena, where eight lions were already waiting, when one of the lions sprang upon him, struck him with the forepaw, and crushed his shoulder with one terrific bite. The scent of blood brought the tigers around him, but Sawade, by a superhuman effort, threw the lion from him and facing the entire fourteen excited beasts, drove them out of the arena, locked the gate, and dropped senseless. He did not perform again for two years, eighteen months of which he spent in hospital.

In the Dutch town of Scheveningen a huge tiger, one born in captivity, leapt upon his head, tore his scalp, and hung on.

125 Alfred Schneider and his Lions

126 The Big Cage, Olympia

His eyes were blinded by the streaming blood, and the other tigers, roused to primitive blood-lust, grew dangerously restive. With the help of his assistant, who had to fire four blank cartridges at the face of the clawing and clinging horror upon his master, Sawade shepherded the excited tigers down the runway before he collapsed. The assistant was Rudolf Matthies, now one of the principal trainers of Hagenbeck's.

Rudolf is one of the most lovable men I know. He has been in the profession for twenty-two years. His simple modesty, his kindliest of natures transmitted to the most ferocious brutes on earth by that subtle radiation which only animal men know, is proclaimed not only by demeanour, but reflected in his face. He is the possessor of a pair of wistful eyes, the broad nose that betokens good-nature, a sensitive mouth and an extremely gentle and sweet voice. That voice is as caressing when talking of the mutual friends abroad in his cosy living-caravan as it is when addressing his four-footed partners in the arena. Tigers are tigers whether they come from Malaya or India, or were born in cages, and, like men, they have their idiosyncrasies and vary in character. The solitary carnivore differs from the beast of prey who hunts with the pack. He has no social sense whatever, and to instil into fifteen savage jungle cats a spirit which holds in suspension the natural proclivity to kill is an achievement of high order. Every creature must be known individually by name; each one has his own peculiar 'kinks.' Rudolf loves his animals. Though they belong to Hagenbeck, they are his protégés, and the product of his patience, his courage and his genius. He has been all over the world, first with bears, then with his favourites, the monstrous painted cats of the primitive East. We have had many adventures together, stirring and amusing, but these will keep for future occasion. His pet tigress at present is named 'Olympia' because she was born there in 1933. I helped to deliver her into the world. Rudolf's greatest hero is his former master and present director, Richard Sawade, and his great ambition in life is to retire one day and rear chickens. He can certainly eat them, for one Christmas night we spent, in German spirit, with Alfred and Frau Kaden, he ate five young chickens at one sitting. Both Matthies and

Kaden are true 'Hagenbeck' men and so was Adolf Kossmeyer. Hagenbeck trainers detest 'slanging' animals and they detest humbug. When a performer spends half his time cracking big whips, shouting and firing off guns, he is no good. He is either a pure humbug or 'yellow' somewhere. Wild animals have a wonderful dignity of their own, and it is a proud privilege to win their confidence and their obedience. Those of my readers who were fortunate enough to witness the performance of Trubka during his stay in England will understand what I mean. Elegance, agility and modest demeanour were all his. He moved in his cage of tigers with the beauty of a ballet dancer and never spoke above a whisper. Trubka knew how much more one can get from an animal by using cajolery instead of threat. One of his tigers was an enormous creature quite as big as the 'Emir' of Matthies. It weighed 550 pounds. This animal attacked him in France some time ago, and we all heard of Trubka's death with great sorrow. The report was wrong, however; he is quite well and back at his work.

Why, if men are gentle and have the animal gift, do animals sometimes attack them? I have already tried to explain why, but let me tell you of one who resembled Trubka very greatly, my dead friend Kossmeyer. Adolf Kossmeyer, whom we called 'Cossmy' for short, was a short, slim, pallid and ascetic-looking young man of twenty-five years. He came with his father Karl, his brother Alphonse, a group of nine Nubian lions, and a group of bears, from Czechoslovakia. One of those bears, a cream-white, silver-haired giant from the Polar ice-fields, tore him to pieces on August 22nd 1930. The last fortnight of his life I spent in his company at Hastings, where the tragedy occurred.

The Kossmeyers have been famous wild-beast trainers for many generations, and Adolf was one of the cleverest of them. Being born to the job, he had no fear, but, like many others, he often had strange misgivings. He confided to me just two days before his lamentable death that he believed Cæsar, the lion, would one day kill him. He had not the slightest premonition that any of his bears, except a huge Russian one, would molest him. Yet bears are very much worse to handle than lions. It is a somewhat gruesome saying in the circus world that bear trainers never retire. In other words, they never get the chance. Sooner or later those morticed teeth and terrible scimitar-like claws get the wariest of men.

In the case of Adolf, the tragedy was the more poignant because unexpected. Only a few hours before it happened, the bear was delicately taking pieces of loaf-sugar from my own lips. It was washing day, and the animals were washed separately in a zinc-floored cage. Zoo authorities used to marvel at the beautiful condition and velvet-like sheen of Cossmy's bears. The secret was a simple one, or intricate one, according to your point of view. Adolf washed his bears with his own hands, using soap-flakes, while his assistant played the hose-pipe on them. Polar bears love the water, and the process of washing always puts them in a good humour. They are clumsy creatures to manipulate in a small cage, however, for they weigh anything from 600 to 1,000 lb. avoirdupois. The Polar bear is the largest carnivore on earth. Not being able to direct the water-jet from every angle, the bear had to be turned round. Adolf pushed its flank with one hand and was pulling its withers with the other when he trod on some soap-flakes lying on the already wet zinc floor. His feet slipped from under him and in falling his elbow caught the bear a severe blow on the snout. Here was the first pain ever inflicted by a gentle master, but the wild beast cannot reason. All the cunning and ferocity hived in that shallow skull from generations of grim, stark struggle in the frozen north, sprang suddenly to activity. The next five minutes were the most horrible I have ever known, for nothing short of death will compel a Polar bear to release its grip until sure of the death of its victim. This dreadful catastrophe sent a thrill of horror through the entire circus world, for young Cossmy was a cultured and lovable personality.

These bald details are harrowing enough, and bring back memories too poignant to accentuate by elaboration. The reader may be interested to know what happens to the wild beast—lion, tiger or bear—after it has killed a trainer.

No one dreams of blaming it. Trainers themselves, and all men who know brute psychology, know perfectly well that such creatures are killers by nature. Their bodily equipment is for killing, and their attacks are the perfectly natural responses to a menacing environment. In this case the menace came from the accidental blow, but a wasp-sting on the bear's nose might just as easily have caused Cossmy's death. Animals that go permanently bad are excluded from a group, but those who act merely from impulse are retained, and never punished for acts they cannot help.

Polar bears are the most dangerous of captive animals, and for several reasons. Unlike lions, tigers, wolves, hyenas, pumas and leopards, all of which are trained to perform, the Polar bear gives no indication of its state of mind. It possesses what the card player calls a 'poker' face. Its expression never changes, and, therefore, one never knows what it will do next. It has more cunning and is infinitely more relentless in its savagery than even the tiger, though it is much slower in action, not being a cat. This is because its habitat, the Arctic tonsure on the head of the world, is merciless itself. There, the struggle for existence is more severe than it is in the desert. The food supply is not only meagre, but enormously difficult to procure.

This environmental influence cannot be eradicated in captivity—it can be temporarily suspended, that is all. Everyone who approaches within striking distance of a Polar bear is in deadly danger—no matter how spotless and innocent-looking the creature might be. To retain a grip upon fish, young seals and young walruses—the most elusive of prey—the Polar bear's teeth are peculiarly fashioned. The law of adaptation has moulded them into the most formidable of weapons. The soles of the feet are covered with hair—the bear does not slip, and he is as silent as he is invisible among the ice and snows of his home region. Added to all these there is his truly tremendous weight—anything from six hundred to one thousand pounds. When those reflexes I have spoken of act—what chance has a puny man? Animal training is the most perilous of all professions, but the most fascinating to one who has faith in himself. *It must not be imagined, however, that every time a trainer or performer is mauled he has been subject to an attack.* The great carnivores are not for ever awaiting

127 An Animal Performance at Olympia

128 Althoff's Elephants at Olympia

some opportunity to kill one. On several occasions the present writer has been very close to death from lions and tigers because they were in *playful* mood. Frank Bostock was nearly killed by a lion because one of his claws got entangled in the lace of his boot. One of the last cage tragedies in Britain was the death of Thomas Purchase, some four years ago, from the 'attack' of a lion. Purchase had an artificial leg and the lion seized it in play, with the result that Purchase overbalanced and fell. Thinking him in trouble, others rushed to drive off the lion. That sealed the fate of poor Purchase, for when a caged lion is scared it is one of the most dangerous animals on earth. There are times when animals are moody like human beings. Toothache and dyspepsia do not make men good-tempered, and animals are not immune to such ills. Possibly half the troubles that take place in the cages of lions, tigers and leopards are due to sex disturbances.

Animals in captivity, as well as in the wild, have their triangle dramas. I know one huge and very handsome Nubian lion who is the essence of good nature until he is conscious of the proximity of a lioness 'in season.' Then he becomes a fiend incarnate and no one dare go even near the bars of his cage. I have ridden on his back and placed my face in his open jaws, with four lionesses looking on. What would have happened had one of those females become 'sexy?' Tolerance of or even affection for kindly man, will not overrule the most powerful impulse of animal nature.

Here is a true and to my mind beautiful story of Matthies and his tigress Julia. She refused point-blank one day to enter the ring after walking up the runway. He was immediately behind her and the other eleven tigers had already entered the arena and were occupying their 'blocks.' Julia lay at the entrance and Matthies stooped to slap her with his hand when she suddenly whirled and seized him by the shoulder, dragging him to the ground. He shouted her name very loudly and she immediately released him. Had anyone got panicky and struck her, Matthies would have been killed outright, but fortunately no one was near enough. Next day Julia died—from pneumonia. Here it is perfectly obvious that the animal was ill and that this was her method of conveying the fact to her trainer. A similar experience was mine some thirty-odd years ago. I worked with a pair of lions, Corsair and Alice, in a wagon cage, and one night the lion was in a most intractable mood. I was worried all night and could not sleep. Next morning I went early to the cage and found Corsair limping very painfully. I went inside, talking sympathetically to the animal, and like a fool, attempted to take hold of his leg. The next moment I was pinned by the thigh with his teeth and my waistcoat ripped to shreds with his claws. Old man Day had always warned me never to move or cry out if a brute 'got me.' He solemnly assured me that a big cat has five jaws, and 'the one he chews with is of the least consequence.' I have always dreaded claws more than teeth, especially the enormously powerful and efficient hook-apparatus of a lion or leopard.

The cat's claw is retractile, worked by a kind of anatomical spring arrangement. It enters the flesh at an angle, but is not withdrawn in the same way. Usually the claw is dirty with decayed horse-flesh, consequently the wound it makes is always septic.

Mercifully, on this occasion, I was absolutely alone in the tent, for any attempt to save me would undoubtedly have been fatal. I never moved, but talked gently until his jaws relaxed, and still talking, I edged away. The beast limped over to the lioness, snarled at her, struck her over the head, and flopped down.

By this time I was outside with nothing more serious than a scratch just below the chest. Corsair still limped at night and performed in a wicked temper. Several times I was scared at him, and was glad to get out.

Next morning we roped him to the bars and discovered an ingrowing claw nearly penetrating the footpad. This is as painful to a lion as an ingrowing toe-nail is to a human being. It is easily put right by simply nipping off the point of the claw a job more easily accomplished to-day by using an anæsthetic on the sufferer.

Apart from the danger arising from an animal suffering pain and unable to tell about it, one has to guard against excitement created by the unusual. I could tell scores of stories to illustrate this point, but one will suffice.

The most dangerous situation I ever found myself in occurred six years ago, in the South of England. I was with the touring circus (Mills's), and before rehearsal with the nine huge lions Kossmeyer, the trainer, took me down the animal tunnel and *forgot I was there*. He opened the doors of the lion cages, entered the first one, stood aside with the wooden fork and called out the lions. They came out literally over my head. I was in a space not more than four feet wide, hemmed in by iron bars, and every one of the nine lions jammed me in turn as they sprang from the cage. Had I been in the middle of the tunnel instead of the cage end of it, I might have been torn to shreds. I was an unfamiliar apparition in an unusual place and the lions immediately became suspicious. That is why training an animal is a slow process. It is all a question of association with familiar things, words and acts, established by bribery and with infinite patience. This training is good for the animals for, of all the deplorable ills, cage-*ennui* is the worst. Look at the typical circus animal and then contrast it with the captive in any zoological gardens. I have already mentioned that zoo officials remarked the beautiful condition and appearance of Adolf Kossmeyer's Polar bears. The following paragraph will help to explain. It was sent out by the Central News Agency on July 7th 1930:

'Philadelphia, Tuesday.

'Dr. Herbert Fox, director of the Laboratory of Comparative Pathology of the Zoological Society of Philadelphia and a member of the University of Pennsylvania, finds that wild animals thrive better in circuses than in zoos, and that the death rate is lower in travelling menageries.

'He attributes this to two main causes. One is that circus trainers are more devoted to their charges than the average zoo keeper and give them more companionship, for which the caged animals crave.

'The other—and more important—reason is that circus animals have continual change of scene and develop a keenness and zest for life entirely lacking in animals in zoos, which have often only the same narrow bit of the world on which to gaze day in and day out.

'Though circus animals are kept when travelling in dark, rough-riding freight-cars, a compensating effect is found in the colourful glitter of the circus when the tents are set up and the show begins.

'"It is true of animals as of human beings," says Dr. Fox, "that monotony kills."'

It is hard to break this human 'companionship' once established. Everyone has heard of the old hunter relegated to the farmer's milk-cart shafts who heard the Tally Ho! of the hunt and dashed off with the cart at his heels. Here is a circus story to match it. John Gindl, one of Hagenbeck's trainers, now in the employment of Bertram Mills, trained six zebras and six mules to perform a 'liberty' act in the ring. This was an extraordinary act, though most people were not aware of it. Five years ago he brought his animals to the Kelvin Hall Circus, run by Mr. Gus Bostock, whose menagerie formed part of the carnival. One morning one of the zebras was found seriously injured in the leg. The lions had roared in chorus (as they usually do) during the night, and this particular zebra had jumped with fright and trapped one of his hind-legs over the stall barrier. I was there that morning and watched the veterinary surgeon at work. He found a nasty wound and dreadfully sprained tendons. The zebra was given additional straw and made as comfortable as possible. The afternoon performance began at two-thirty and the zebra and mule act was timed for an hour later. Gindl had to enter the ring with six mules and five zebras. The grooms took down the trappings and prepared the animals for their entrance, leaving the wounded zebra lying at ease on the straw. The timid creature made no movement until from the circus band came the 'zebra music,' then a transformation took place. The frantic struggles of that animal to rise and make for the ring were positively pathetic.

All the wild animals of the circus, as well as the horses, know the music of their own act and it invariably excites them. They are as impatient to perform as the human stars who

129 George Power's Elephants

130 Bertram Mills' Elephants

131 Elsie Wallenda

132 'God Save the King'

wait for their cue behind the curtains. The most conceited, if I dare use that word, are bears and chimpanzees. It is very difficult at times to get them out of the ring, and when left alone they will carry through a performance of their own.

I might observe that, with very few exceptions, wild animals are not taught to do anything 'unnatural' in the way of posture. In nature lions and tigers sit and stand, and paw the air. They jump over bushes and through apertures in tangled thorn, and when man-eaters, they will jump over a blazing fire to seize a native and carry him off. They also roll over on sand and rock, and bear one another's weight in their gambols. Polar bears who climb a staircase and then slide down a wooden chute are only emulating their wild brethren on the ice-floes and hillocks of the north. They are asked to do nothing more than these simple tricks in the circus, and they not only enjoy doing them, but the performance does them a world of good.

It is not the tricks themselves that matter. *What really matters is the presence of a man or woman in a cage of lions or other jungle lords.* When Clement Merk, for instance, lies down on a divan with nothing more than bathing drawers on, places a raw steak on his naked body, and calls Judy the lioness to come over and eat it there—it is Merk who suffers discomfiture, not Judy. Clement travels with the Sanger circus but he has been with others all over the world. His assistant was killed by a lion in South America and, in his efforts to save him, Clement lost a fragment of his skull from the lion's claws. He has had his head trepanned.

Sea-lions are always a delight to a circus audience. Even Carl Hagenbeck the elder was astounded when Joseph Woodward first trained some to perform. Carl thought Woodward an American. He was an Englishman and died only three years ago at Ramsgate. His sons toured with sea-lions for many years and trained some remarkable animals. To-day there are many of these animal comedians delighting circus audiences in Britain, on the Continent and in America. Elsie Wallenda yokes one in a chariot and is drawn from the ring by him. Roland Wesley has taught two of his to play the National Anthem on trumpets fixed together 'pan-pipe' fashion. These animals actually blow the trumpets, they do not push motor-horn bulbs. They are screamingly funny, for one of them makes blunders on purpose and then 'jazzes' the tune. Sea-lions, like all other animals, have to be trained or taught to do their tricks. They are not, as many people think, 'born' jugglers.

I would like to write much more about performing animals and their trainers and tricks. I would like to explode more theories, banish more illusions and destroy the many superstitions which have gathered around such performances. I have not even mentioned elephants. One cannot picture a circus without elephants, can one? I shall have something to say about them in the next chapter.

XI
THE CIRCUS IN AMERICA

THE circus in America dates from 1785 when Ricketts established his little show at Philadelphia.

In 1793 it was patronised by George Washington. Tenting circuses began in 1826, and combinations of circus and menagerie in 1851. Readers interested in details of these early efforts will find material in R. W. G. Vail's *Random Notes of the History of the Early American Circus*.

To-day the U.S.A. is the home of the big circus, and that began really when P. T. Barnum entered partnership with Coup and Costello. Barnum's show was the 'greatest show on earth' and probably the greatest that ever has been. It was Coup, however, and not Barnum, who first negotiated with the railroad companies to transport the great show by rail. Barnum even protested, desiring the old road transport. This was in 1872.

What prodigious workers these men were! Coup worked out the transport arrangements to such perfection that the huge combination of museum, freak collection, menagerie and circus could travel one hundred miles each night, have a parade through the streets in the morning, and present both afternoon and evening performances.

Phineas Taylor Barnum was born on July 5th 1810 at Danbury, in Fairfield, Connecticut. He died of congestion of the brain on April 7th 1891 in his eighty-first year. He was a grocer, a clerk, editor of the paper (the *Herald of Freedom*) for which he was jailed, and a showman.

He dabbled in local politics, was religious, but had no conscience, although he was harmless. He was the greatest humbug, fraud and liar of his age, and possibly the most audacious publicist and spoof-merchant who ever lived.

Barnum was imposed upon many a time, but he always made money out of it. The old Negro woman, Joice Heth, whom he bought for one thousand dollars and exhibited as

George Washington's nurse, was only eighty years old, but she was not a runaway slave. He bought her with all the forged credentials from R. W. Lindsay, a showman who described her as being 190 years of age. She died and was 'respectably' buried by Barnum, who knew she was a fraud from the beginning.

The bearded lady he exhibited was Madame Clofullia, and she was quite genuine. Barnum had freaks on the brain. He collected india-rubber men, living skeletons, legless and armless humans, giants, dwarfs, midgets (there is a difference), and all sorts of creatures with more limbs or less than nature customarily provides. 'General Tom Thumb,' whose proper name was Charles Stratton, was found by Barnum's brother in Bridgeport. He was a child of five, but Barnum passed him off as eleven years of age, brought him to England and presented him to Queen Victoria.

When this midget was twenty-five, Barnum made a show of his wedding to Miss Lavinia Warren, another midget. They were married on February 10th 1863. There was a fearful rumpus about it all, but Barnum made publicity even out of the row, and told one fastidious lady who threatened to 'expose' him by writing a pamphlet to 'print a hundred thousand copies stating I stole the communion plate after the ceremony; then come to me and I will estimate the money value of your services to me as an advertising agent.'

President Lincoln almost fell in love with Lavinia Warren because she resembled his wife. Lavinia's sister Minnie married 'Commodore Nutt,' and Barnum had all four midgets on show at once. I have a photograph signed by these two in my possession which they presented to my own mother when Minnie was in London.

In 1850 Barnum succeeded in persuading Jenny Lind, the 'Swedish Nightingale,' to come to New York. The six New York concerts alone realised over eighty-seven thousand dollars. Jenny travelled America for some two years, her personality winning everyone and disarming all criticism. Her popularity was beginning to decline after she left Barnum, but Barnum was her defender ever—even after her death. 'She was a woman who would have been adored if she had

133 An American 'Lay-out'

134 The Death of Jumbo

the voice of a crow,' he once said. However, Jenny has no part in circus history.

In 1873 the Barnum circus added another ring—the first two-ring circus in the world. Other American circuses followed suit. Then came the three-ring circus, and to-day the four-ring is contemplated. This kind of show is detested in Britain. No spectator can watch three different performances at once, and if he attempts to concentrate on one the others cause so much distraction that his enjoyment is ruined. In America, the land of hustle, it is necessary to get an entire population accommodated during one day's stay. Accordingly the huge tent is constructed to hold fifteen thousand spectators and all of them see a complete circus performance but by no means the entire performance of the circus.

Barnum's greatest circus rivals were Cooper and Bailey. Later Cooper, Bailey and Hutchinson's 'Great London Circus, Sanger's Royal British Menagerie, and International Allied Shows,' captured much patronage from Barnum. Barnum was rattled, more especially when his rivals began to boom their baby elephant—born on tour.

In 1880 an agreement was entered into and the shows combined. Such was the beginning of the world-famous 'Barnum and Bailey.' James Anthony Bailey, whose real name was McGinnis, was born in Detroit, Michigan, on July 4th 1847. He was Barnum's junior by thirty-seven years. In character he was Barnum's superior to an incalculable degree. A strict teetotaller, shrewd business man, an organising genius of the first water and possessing an overplus of nervous energy, he carried the entire business on his shoulders. Unlike his more spectacular partner, Bailey hated humbug, fraud, deceit and even publicity. The sight of his own photograph on a poster made him positively ill. 'How I would hate to have him for a rival,' once said Barnum. Barnum and Bailey were a wonderful pair, and they made glorious circus history. Bailey, however, was the better man of the two. He died in 1906 from the effects of an insect bite. The greatest single business deal they brought off during their partnership was the purchase of Jumbo, the huge African elephant, from the London Zoological Society. The credit for this transaction must be given to Barnum, who saw Jumbo many times in London. When the Society agreed to sell him for ten thousand dollars Barnum was both surprised and delighted. The publicity he got made him more delighted still. Jumbo had become a London institution, and to send him off to an American showman was a trifle worse than sacrilege and treason combined. To the public it was like disposing of St. Paul's Cathedral to a vulgar American quack religionist. Lords, knights, squires, artists—even Queen Victoria, the Prince of Wales and John Ruskin, besides thousands of petitioners—tried to save Jumbo from Barnum. Questions were asked in Parliament, and an attempt was made to secure an injunction to prevent the Zoo from selling him. Barnum won his Jumbo, however, and the great African elephant was duly carted off to America. What the British public were not told was that Jumbo was becoming dangerous and the Zoo officials were glad to see the back of him. When he reached America the reception was amazing. All New York now went Jumbo mad. Barnum had advertised him as the veritable Mastodon—the only one on earth.

The mighty elephant did not last long. On September 15th 1885 Jumbo was struck by a goods train which he derailed. He was pinned between the wreckage and the show train, suffered a skull fracture and died in a moment. Barnum had had him just over three years. Two years later the show's winter quarters were destroyed by fire and every animal, except thirty elephants and one lion, killed. In six hours Barnum had purchased by cable enough animals for a new menagerie. He established permanent quarters at the old Madison Square Garden, and from here in 1889 the Barnum and Bailey Circus came to Olympia, London. It was a great success and returned the following year. In that year Barnum died at the age of eighty, a millionaire.

On the show's last visit to this country a few years later the tour did not pay, and on returning to America it was taken over by the celebrated Ringling Brothers. There were originally six brothers, but only one, John, now survives. In 1918 the two shows were combined and are now run with three rings, four stages and some eight hundred performers

135 America: Names to conjure with

136 America: Stables of the Work Horses

137 America: An entire Town Population can be seated in Ringling's

(animal and human) at Madison Square Garden, New York. Every great artist has performed at the 'Ringling Brothers and Barnum and Bailey Circus.' It is hard to realise that this gigantic show can take the road and travel for thousands of miles without a hitch of any importance in the programme—so perfect is the organisation. Every act at Ringlings is a 'Display,' and there are usually some twenty-two displays on the programme. Many of these, however, take place simultaneously, so that it is impossible for anyone to see the entire programme. The opening spectacle is one of bewildering splendour and takes the form of some famous incident of pageantry such as the 'Durbar of Delhi' or 'Field of the Cloth of Gold.' The trappings, costumes and array of animals and performers, are as impressive as they are wonderful. The last season's programme was a staggering one. It included Miss Dorothy Herbert riding her stallion through fire and performing many other audacities, without reins; the Flying Concellos; the Flying Comets; the Otari Troupe; the Wallendas; the Walter Guice Family; the Loyal-Repenski Family; and the Rieffenachs. Any one of these acts would fill Olympia, yet they are but a few from one programme of twenty-two 'Displays.' Around the hippodrome track an entire family of rare pygmy African elephants was marched. These animals are the rarest of all elephants. Like human pygmies they are of dwarfed stature—miniatures of the largest of all terrestrial mammals.

America has always had a fondness for elephants, and the best elephant trainers have been schooled either at Barnum and Bailey's or Ringlings. One thinks of Conklin, Wallace Beery (the great film actor, who was Ringling's elephant or 'bull' man) and of Power, the stepfather of George O'Brien, who is the master of any of them.

George O'Brien (Power) was with Ringlings for years before he went on his world tour. His mother Jeannette Power was the wife of John O'Brien, Barnum's celebrated horse trainer. Jeannette herself was a famous high school performer and beauty. She figured on the programme as Miss Tonelli, and first came to this country with the Barnum show on the occasion of its last visit. Her husband trained her mounts. He was a wizard with horses, and once beat all Continental Carousels by training seventy horses to perform in the ring at once. He directed them from the centre, mounted upon a coal-black stallion elevated on a circular drum. His pretty wife was a superb rider who seldom used her reins, and sat on a side-saddle. Jenny had scores of admirers who were not aware of her married state. A young artist of the period, Charles Dana Gibson, a brother-in-law of the present vivacious Lady Astor, took her for one of his models. The 'Gibson Girl' period, which will be remembered by members of the last generation, marked an advance in feminine fashion towards the picturesque.

When John O'Brien died, she married Power, the elephant trainer, who, according to an eminent European authority, 'topped the pinnacle so far as elephant training was concerned.' George O'Brien, who uses the name Power, is one of the cleverest elephant trainers in the world. His four huge animals do the most amazing things, including intricate dances, telephone conversations and sham fights. One of them, the smallest member of an extremely amusing and clever quartette, originally travelled with Frank Bostock, who was known in America as the 'Animal King.'

Frank was the brother of my friend E. H. Bostock, the English menagerist, and his one-time partner. He went to America and became the owner of a huge menagerie in which the greatest animal trainers of that continent performed. Among these were Herman Weedon, John Gentner (Jack Bonavita), Madame Morelli of leopard fame, and Madame Pianka. Frank himself was a remarkable trainer and a great showman. He had both the appearance and the brains of the successful showman, being well-built, handsome, and having a genius for inventing publicity stunts.

He was the author of a well-written work, *The Training of Wild Animals*, the system expounded therein being somewhat different from the Hagenbeck method but equally gentle. Frank travelled Europe several times, his last appearance in the cage being in 1905, when he was attacked by the celebrated lion 'Wallace' in Paris and had to go to hospital for several weeks. When he died, his great collection of animals was dispersed, many of the lions going to Charles Gay, who used them to stock a lion farm near Los Angeles, California.

Mr. Charles Gay was originally a Bostock trainer and conceived the idea of training lions for film purposes. The Bostock lions were useless to the movie people because they had been trained to perform definite tricks. Gay set to work and bred lions *which he trained to act*. Instead of the usual circus tricks they were taught to leap, spring upon human dummies without damaging them, and to express or 'register' annoyance and rage. One of his best animals, possibly the best-trained lion the world has ever known, was Numa, who died a few years ago. Numa earned as much as £2,000 in one year.

No lion is safe with human beings, and whenever one sees lions on the films one can be sure the trainer is near. Sometimes a glass screen, which does not photograph, separates the actors from the animals. Mr. Gay 'grades' his lions by weeding out the inveterate savages, but even the quiet ones cannot be trusted too much. Only last year one of his men, Herman Ziegler, was set upon by eighteen lions and torn to pieces. Ziegler was a very able trainer, and the tragedy was the ghastliest Gay's establishment had known. The cause of this dreadful accident was a simple one. Ziegler stumbled over an upturned pedestal and fell upon his back. The 'cats' saw the recumbent 'mouse' and immediately sprang upon it. They simply could not resist the instinct to destroy the moving object which had ceased (in their eyes) to be a man. Such, again, is cat psychology.

There are other schools in America, the Goebels' school, for example, where not only animals are trained for circus work, but performers also. Many of the best animal-exhibitors, however, have been men and women who had a native genius for the work. Mabel Stark and her tigers was an act to marvel at, but Mabel was severely mauled about two years ago and I have not heard of her for some time. Clyde Beatty, who was attached to Ringling Brothers and Barnum and Bailey Circus, and to the Hagenbeck-Wallace Circus (under Ringling's supervision), is the leading animal performer in America. He now tours with his own circus in partnership with the

Coles. Beatty is a young man still, very daring and spectacular, but he has a lot to learn about lions and tigers. A course of instruction under men like Sawade or Willy Peters would do him no harm.

Lions and tigers are quite plentiful, and it is certainly not necessary to fasten one down to a staple in the floor by a collar and chain-cable in order to 'train' it. That is not winning its confidence but torturing it with pain and fear. When Mr. Beatty says this is only done 'with specially ferocious animals' he makes a foolish admission, for no intelligent trainer would attempt to train a 'specially ferocious' lion or tiger. It isn't worth the candle, for such an animal will inevitably spoil an act by misbehaviour. Nor is it true, as the film exhibition of the Beatty act stated, that 'Clyde Beatty is the first man to bring lions and tigers together in the same cage.' Sawade did this long before Beatty was born, and Bostock and Wombwell's were showing performing lions and tigers in a mixed group half a century ago.

The Al. G. Barnes' Circus tours the Pacific coast and seldom comes east of Kansas. It is one of the most popular of American circuses. That old favourite of the Western film dramas, Tom Mix, now also has a circus of his own; he was a circus performer before he took to film work. Tom's circus is not a very imposing affair, but his personality still counts, and so far his show has been a success. Another cowboy film star touring with a show is Ken Maynard. It is not a circus, however, but a miniature of the famous Wild West spectacle associated with the name of Buffalo Bill.

The Sells–Floto, Lewis Brothers Circus, and Sylvan–Drew Circus, are three very good shows which maintain high standard programmes year after year and cover thousands of miles of territory. There is now a Community Circus in Gainesville with one hundred and fifty performers, not one of whom is a professional. In the present season they have no fewer than twenty displays on the programme. American circuses have improved in many respects, not the least improvement being the abolition of the army of grafters they once tolerated. These rogues were in many cases attached to the circus staff and their job was to rook the public with

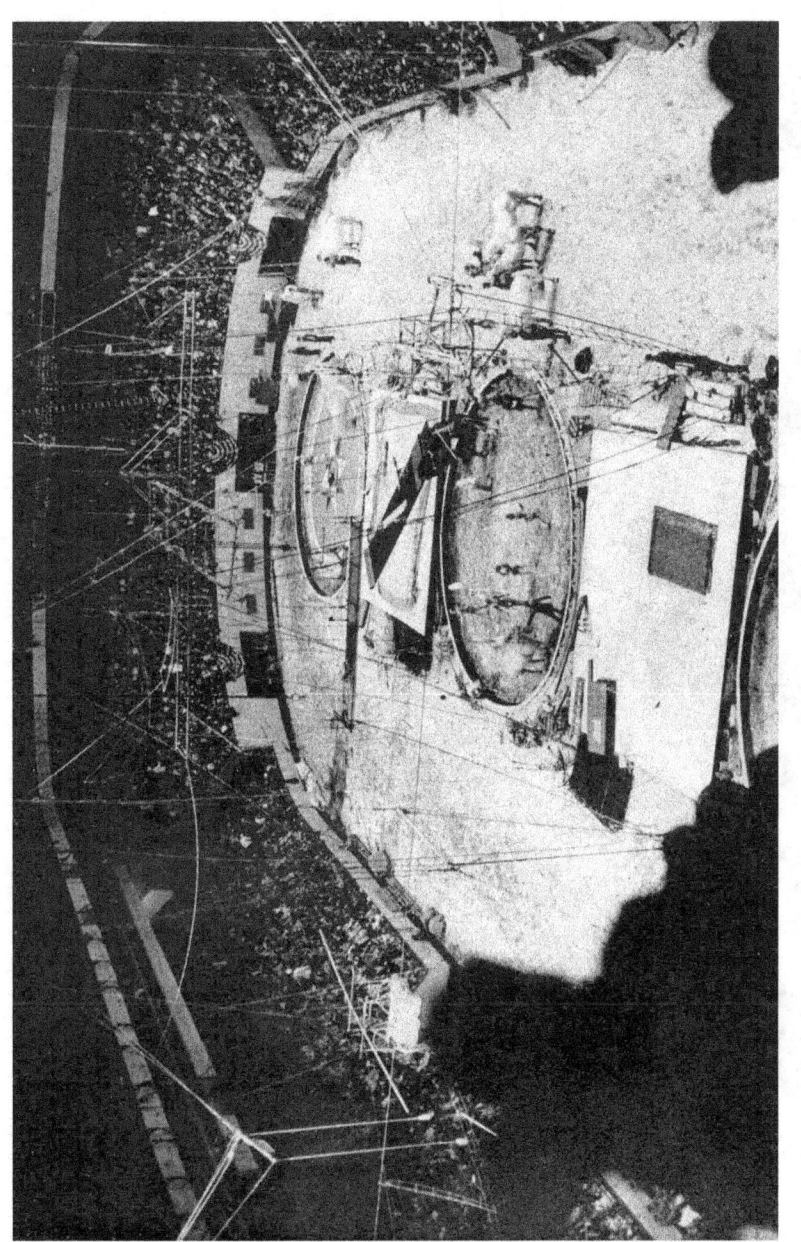
138 An American 'Three-Ring, Three-Stage' Circus

139 'Over the Bridge.' In this Act a perfect sense of Balance is combined with great muscular Strength

THE CIRCUS IN AMERICA

quack medicines, fake jewellery and dishonest side-shows. Many an old-time circus was burned to the ground by a justifiably resentful mob. In those days the sinister cry of 'Hey Rube!' was the rallying call of the showmen, who came to one another's assistance armed with any weapon they could seize, from an elephant whip to a colt. 'Hey Rube!' is now quite extinct, for the American circuses are run by men of high integrity whose aim is certainly to make money but who believe the best way to make it is to give good value for it.

It is, perhaps, hardly permissible to introduce a Wild West Show and Congress of Rough Riders of the World, into a book on the Circus. Anything touching show-life in America, however, does not seem complete without mention of that most picturesque figure the show-world ever produced—Buffalo Bill.

He certainly touches the fringe of British circus history, for it was through his law suit with George Sanger that that volatile person assumed the lordly title. I met Buffalo Bill when I was little more than a boy. His great show was in my town and I not only saw the performance twice, but I talked with the great showman, with Johnny Baker, and with the Indian Chief called Sitting Bull. In these days I am inclined to believe that the Sitting Bull I spoke to was a fraud, for the victor of the Little Big Horn battle died in 1890.

William Frederick Cody was a very handsome man with a very nasal voice. He was born in Iowa on February 26th 1846, and was just two years the junior of my own father, who had patronised his show on its previous visit to England. Among those who attended it on that occasion were Queen Victoria, her son and grandson (afterwards King Edward and King George) and Mr. Gladstone.

Cody, when I saw his show, rode a beautiful white horse but took a very small part in the performance. I remember his canter down the field when his 'Congress' had been called together, the sweeping gesture with his sombrero, and his loudly roared speech: 'Ladies and Gentlemen! I beg to introduce to you my celebrated rough-riders of the world.' These consisted of groups of Redskins, Cowboys, Gauchos,

Arabs, Boers, Cossacks and United States Cavalrymen. Exhibitions of different styles of rough-riding followed, each group having the arena to itself. The great Bill himself did nothing but shoot and bring down white balls thrown into the air by a rider some paces ahead of him. As he was probably using duck-shot cartridges there was nothing extraordinary in his act. Followed scenes from the pony-express days, and an Indian attack on the original Deadwood Coach (this identical coach is now in possession of Mr. Bertram Mills).

I remember Johnny Baker, who was a marvellous shot, introduced a thrill which would be laughed at nowadays. He rode down an inclined plane on one of the first motor-cycles and leapt a chasm several yards wide—landing upon a wooden platform amid the tumultuous cheers of the audience.

Cody was a one-time scout, a colonel in the American army, and an employee of the Kansas Pacific Railroad Company. 'Employee' is a curious word with which to describe a man whose specific job was to kill bison in order to feed the railroad workers on the prairie. He slaughtered so many in one year that he earned his celebrated nickname, 'Buffalo Bill'. The Sioux Indians called him 'Pa-he-heska' (the long-haired).

He married Louisa Federci in 1866. Col. William F. Cody was a friend of General Sheridan's, and it was Sheridan who appointed him Chief of Scouts. He was persuaded to become a showman by August Belmont, Anson Steger and James Gordon Bennett, and produced his first public show at Omaha, Nebraska. He was a fine, upright, manly fellow, and though much rubbish has been written about him, no one has ever said a mean thing of him. He died at Denver, Colorado, on January 10th 1917.

XII
CONCLUSION

In writing this description (I cannot call it a history) of a wonderful institution and a great profession I have been very happy. I have lived again with old comrades human and animal, the living and the dead. Old scenes have been resurrected, old and exciting incidents re-lived, and old friendships revived.

Observation, study, but above all experience, are the writer's chief aids, and because I have depended mostly upon experience I believe I have succeeded in avoiding the meretricious in this book on the Circus. To the stars, themselves, many of whom are not mentioned, I am indebted for much instruction. Stars alone make neither the heavens nor the circus, however. There are others upon whom the limelight shines but dimly or not at all, but without whose services the show could not go on. To the organisers, business managers, publicity agents, equestrian directors, bandmasters, grooms and ring-boys I am equally indebted. The success or failure of the show depends very largely upon the first three; the success of the entertainment upon the second two; and the smoothness of the performances upon the last two.

The duties of the Equestrian Director are very exacting. He has his time-schedule to draw up and he has to be ever in attendance to see that his performers adhere to it. Willy Schumann (who died while this book was in the press), Archie Pearson (the doyen of ringmasters), Leicester Cooke, Frank Foster, Frank Ginett, and that veteran horse-master, Major Arthur Sowler, have never been too busy or too harassed to offer me assistance when in difficulties. These gentlemen know the technique of circus work from alpha to omega. The Bandmaster of the circus is a more highly skilled person than his music leads one to believe. Here again, the circumstances are bizarre. Sir Thomas Beecham would be a complete failure in the bandstand at Olympia; he would conduct for human enjoyment. Jack Lindsley, the cleverest band-conductor we have, knows just precisely *what the animals in the ring will respond to*. Believe me, there is all the difference in the world. Very frequently his music must follow the movements in the ring. This is infinitely more difficult than playing for people or animals *who follow the music*. Jack gets many a headache but he never loses either his nerve or his temper.

To Captain J. Russel Pickering, Mr. Wallace Gibson and Miss A. A. Moore I am deeply indebted for many kindnesses. The work entailed in knitting so vast a number of people and animals into a homogeneous combination, which is theirs, calls for the highest qualities in men and women. Lastly, I want to thank Mr. Stanley Franklin for his many hospitalities, Messrs. A. S. Williamson and Charles Leighton for their revelations on circus publicity, and Mr. Gus Bostock for the valuable information and advice he is always ready to give with such enthusiasm. May they all flourish.

INDEX

(The numerals in italic denote the *figure numbers* of illustrations)

Abu Zeyd, *quoted*, 27
Adams, Charles, 58
Alberty, 38, 43, 44; *65, 67*
Alfredos, the, 64
Allisons, the, 50, 64; *96*
Althoff's Baby Elephants, *128*
Amburgh, Van, 14, 81, 82, 83, 89
Amor, 51
Anderton & Rowland Day's Menagerie, 81
Ankner, Captain, 28
Antonnet, 62
Armstrong, Archie, 55
Asgards, the, 64
Asra, Madame, 69
Astley's, 6, 7, 8, 9, 10, 11, 12, 13, 14, 28, 30, 34, 56, 70, 82, 83; *6, 7*
Astor, Lady, 58, 110
Atkins, 70, 80, 82
'Augustes,' 56, 57, 61; *70, 72*
Austins, 15, 63
Author, the, 2, *14, 108, 109, 110, 111, 122*

Bailey, J. A., 14, 107
Baker Boys, the, 48, 49; *47, 50*
Baker, Johnny, 113, 114
Ballard, 81
Balzer Sisters, 67; *90*
Banks, 5, 6
Bannister, 10, 11
Barham, R. H., 28
Barnes' Circus, 112
Barnum, P. T., 14, 105, 106, 107
Barnum & Bailey, 47, 58, 107, 108, 109, 111; *135*
Barth, H., 31

Bartholomew Fair, 5, 6, 11, 45, 80, 81
Bartoni, Fritzi, 65
Batty, 10, 14, 82
Baucher, 29, 30
'Bearded Lady,' the, 106
Beasy, Bob, 63
Beatty, Clyde, 87, 111, 112
Beecham, Sir Thomas, 115
Beery, Wallace, 109
Belling, Tom, 57
Belmont, A., 114
Bennett, J. G., 114
Biddall, 58
Blackbourne, Doreen, 35
Blackpool Tower Circus, 61; *73*
'Blondin.' *See* Gravelot, Emile
Bombayo, 66, 67
Bonavita, 93
Bostock's Menagerie, 15, 18, 19, 48, 69, 80, 81, 90, 102, 110, 111; *114*
Bostock & Wombwell's Menagerie, 18, 21, 81, 88, 89, 112; *118, 119*
Boswell's, 15
Boucicault, Dion, 14
Bourgeois, 51
Braham's Menagerie, 81
Bright, Helen, 83; *117*
Briloff family, 14
Brumbach. *See* Sandwina
Buckland, Frank, *quoted*, 83
'Buffalo Bill,' 17, 68, 112, 113, 114
Bulloch, Dr. John, 14
Burchardt-Footit, 31
Burns, 72

Burt, 7
Buschs, 15, 31

Cadman, 41
Campas, 73
Canero, 31
Carlton Sisters, 69
Carres, 15, 28, 31
Carsons, 68
Carter, 82, 89
Chadwicks, 15
Chaplin, Charlie, 57, 58, 65; *81*
Chapman, Nellie, 82, 83
Charles I, 55
Chiarinis, 15
Chipperfield's Menagerie, 81
Christiani Family, 33, 34
Cinquevalli, 45, 69
Clarkes, the, 11, 15
Clarkonians, the, 39
Clemenceau, 30
Clermont, Jean, 47, 48
Clofullia, Madame. *See* 'Bearded Lady'
Coady, Harry, 29
'Coco,' *75*
Codonas, the, 38, 39, 51, 52, 60
Cody, S. F., 47
Cody, William. *See* 'Buffalo Bill'
Coleman, 16
Coles, 15, 112
Colleanos, the, 38, 64, 65; *57, 92, 93, 94*
Colosseum, the, 2
'Commodore Nutt,' 106
Community Circus, 112
Concellos, the, 38, 39, 109; *60*
Conklin, 109

Connaught, Prince Arthur of, 91
Cookes, the, 11, 14, 15, 28, 40, 115
Cooper, Bailey and Hutchinson, 107
Cooper, John, 88, 89
Costello, 62
Cossmy, Adolf, *122, 123*
Coup and Costello, 105
'Couriers,' 39, *43*
Court, Alfred, 94
Craston, Joe, 63
Crocketts, the, 15, 83, 89; *116*
Cromwell, 56
Cross's Exeter 'Change, 70, 80; *115*
Cruikshank, 15
Crystal Palace, the, 42
Cubanos, the, 38, 65, 66

Dal Paos Troupe, 68
Darby, William, 14, 58
Davenant, Sir William, 5
Davis, 9
Delfin, Theodore, 62; *70*
Dellah, William, 89, 90
De Luca Sisters, 97
Dickens, Charles, 28
'Doodles,' 61; *85*
Dratsas, the, *83*
Drury Lane, 58
Ducrows, 11, 14, 27, 34, 35, 70, 82
Dutton, 51

Edmunds, Mr. and Mrs., 80, 81
Edward VII, 89, 108, 113
Elliot, General, 7

Fairgrieve, 81
Fanque, Pablo, 58
Federci, Louisa, 114
'Fiery Jack,' 63
Fillis, James, 29, 30, 31
Fischer, Oscar, 31
'Five Carlos,' the, 50

Flaminius Circus, 2
Florian, Jean, 69
'Flying Comets,' 109
'Flying Dutchman.' *See* Cubanos
'Flying Pass,' *58*
Forepaugh's, 58
Fossett, 15
Foster, Frank, 115
Fox, Dr. Herbert, 101, 102
France, Anatole, 69
Franconis, the, 8, 15
Franks, 15
Fratellini, the, 65
Freeman, James, 16, 60
Frilli, 64
Frost, 7, 41, 82

Gautiers, the, 15
Gay, Charles, 111
Gayton, 51
'General Tom Thumb,' 106
Gentner, John, 110
Gerbola, Tony, 63
Gibson, Charles Dana, 110
Ginnetts, 15, 16, 115
Gladstone, Mr., 113
Glaister, Prof. John, 58
Goebels' School, 111
'Gold Dust Twins,' 67; *98*
Gravelet, Emile, 38, 41, 42; *68, 69*
Griffin, 7
Grimaldi, Joseph, 8, 54, 57, 58, 59
Gindl, John, 102
Grock, 45, 54, 62; *82*

Hadji, Ali, *91*
Hagenbeck's Circus, 15, 35, 36, 84, 87, 91, 95, 96, 102, 103, 110, 111; *26, 113*
Hanneford Family, 60
Harper, 51
Harris, Sir Augustus, 58
Haupt, Carl, 94
Hegelmanns, 38
Henglers, 10, 11, 14, 15, 58, 61

Hilton's Menagerie, 81, 82, 88
Hobbes, 51
Hogarth, 41; *9*
Holloway's Circus, 11
Hone, 80
Hood, Tom, 28
Hoppers, the, 47
Huckle, Amy, *43*
Hughes, 7, 8
Humboldt, 73, 74
Huxter, Percy, 63; *29*

Jacksons, the, 51, 68; *86, 106*
James II, 55
Jamrach's Menagerie, 83
Jarvey, 83
Jeffreys, Judge, 56
'Jenny,' *14*
Jesserich, Albert, 28, 31
Jevons, 58
'Joey,' 57
Johnson, Dr., *quoted*, 9
Jones, 7
Jonson, Ben, 5
Judge, Charles, 16
Julia, Roxie, Jenny and Lena, 23
'Jumbo,' 107, 108; *134*
'Jumping the Balloons,' *41*

Kaden, Alfred, 94, 95, 96
Kayes' Menagerie, 81
Kean, Edmund, 11
Kelvin Hall Circus, 48, 49, 102
Kemmys, the Four, *11*
Knies, 15
Knight, Charles, 4
Kober, Dr., 31, 47
Kossmeyers, the, 28, 31, 94, 96, 97, 98, 101; *34, 53*
Krembsers, the, 15
Krone, 15
Kruger National Park, 72

Lai Foun Troupe, 68; *30*

INDEX

Lawrence Sisters, 38
Lehmann Kara. *See* Cinquevalli, Paul
Leitzel, Lilian, 51
Lewis Brothers Circus, 112
'Liberty Horses,' *8, 37, 41, 42*
Lincoln, President, 106
Lind, Jenny, 106, 107
Lindsay, R. W., 106
Lindsley, Jack, 116
Lippizans, 23, 27, 37; *40*
'Little Leslie,' 63
'Little Tich,' 61
Livy, 1
Lloyd George, Mr., 58
Lockhart's, 15, 91
Loyal-Repenski Family, 109; *49*
Luisita, *61*
Lupino Family, 41

McAllister, William. *See* 'Doodles'
McCarthy, 89, 90
Macartes, the, 15
Maccomo, 89, 90
Mack, Jimmy, 63
'Magyars,' 64
'Manchester Jack,' 81
Mander's Menagerie, 81, 89
Manzano, 31; *52*
Marcelle Golden Statues, *74*
Marie Antoinette, 8
Marshall, 58
Marx, Karl, 58
Maschinos, 64
Matania, F. *5*
Matthies, Rudolf, 94, 95, 96, 99
Mayer, Charley, 62; *70*
Maynard, Ken, 112
Maysy and Brach, 67; *104, 105*
Maximus, Circus, 2
Medrano Sisters, 32; *3, 33, 46, 54*
Menander, 56
Menelik, Emperor, 92, 93
'Merry Andrew,' 54
Merk, Clement, 103
Miller, 7

Mills, Bertram, 21, 27, 35, 37, 48, 49, 50, 58, 62, 67, 70, 101, 102, 114; *18, 23, 31, 41, 42, 130*
Mills, Cyril and Bernard, 22
Milton's Circus, 11
Mix, Tom, 112
Mroczkovski, 28, 29, 30, 37; *38, 40*
Muller, 51
Munthe, Axel, 75

Nubilor, M. Fulvius, 1

O'Brien, George and John, 109, 110
Oliveras, 42
Olympia, Circus at, 2, 22, 31, 48, 49, 58, 69, 70, 91, 108, 109; *13, 51, 52, 126, 127, 128*
Otari Troupe, 109

Pace, 55
Paetzolds, 67
Pagliacci, 46
Palladium, the, 11
'Pas-de-Deux,' *44*
Paulo, 15
Paullus, Lucius Æmilius, 2
Pavlova, 23
Pearson, Archie, 115; *35*
Pederson, Anders, 16
Pepys, *quoted*, 5
Perezofis, the, 69
Peters, Willy, 91, 94, 112
Petoletti Family, 31, 35, 36
Philpotts, Eden, *quoted*, 71
Pianka, Madame, 110
Pickering, Captain J. Russell, 116
Pidcock and Polito's Menagerie, 80; *115*
'Pimpo,' 42, 60; *84*
Pinders, the, 15
Pinocchio, 63
Pompeii, *4*

Poposhill, 51
Powells, the, 15
Power, 109, 110; *129*
Price, 7
Price and Powell's Circus, 11
Purchase, Thomas, 99

Rahere, 45
Raleigh, Sir Walter, 5
Rastelli, 45, 69; *99*
Reeve, Arthur, 16
Renz, 15
Renz, Thereze, 31
Richard, 51
Rickett's Circus, 14
Ricketts, 105
Rieffenachs, the, 109
Ringling Brothers, 14, 108, 109, 111; *135, 137*
Risling Acrobats, 50, 64, 68; *98*
Rivels, Charley, 58, 65
Roberts, David, 10
Roman Circus, the, 2, 3; *5*
Ruskin, John, 108

Salamonsky's, 15
Salerno, 69
Samson, 7
Samwell's Circus, 11
Sandwina, 46, 47
Sanger's Circus, 16, 17, 18, 19, 20, 21, 42, 59, 60, 103; *15*
Sanger Family, 14, 15, 16, 21, 60
Sanger, 'Lord' George, 14, 16, 17, 18, 19, 20, 21, 60, 83, 113; *15, 16, 17*
Sargano. *See* Dellah, William
Sarrasini, 15, 47
Sasha, *75*
Saunders, 10, 11
Sawade, Richard, 91, 94, 95, 112
Schilling, Fritz, 91
Schneider, Alfred, 94; *125*
Schneider's Circus, *25*
Schreiber, Baptista, 31

Schumanns, the, 15, 28, 115; *18, 48*
Scipio, 2
Scogan, 55
Sedgewick's Menagerie, 81
Seeth, Julius, 91, 92, 93, 94; *120, 121*
Sells-Floto Circus, 112
Shakespeare, 5
Sheltons, the, 15
Sheridan, General, 114
'Simba,' 2
'Sitting Bull,' 113
Sloan Family. *See* Yelding Family
Smith, Prof. Elliott, 69
Sobieska, Clementina, 7, 8
Somers, Will, 55
Southwark Fair, 41; *9*
Sowler, Major Arthur, 115
'Speedy,' 63
Springboard acrobats, *10*
Stark, Mabel, 111
Steger, Anson, 114
Strassburger, 15
Stratton, Charles. *See* 'General Tom Thumb'
Strutt, *quoted*, 4
Sue, Eugene, 82
Sulla, 1
Swallow, John, 42

Sylvan-Drew Circus, 112

Tamara, 65
Tarleton, 55
Tarquinius, 2
Teddy, 46
Tennyson, 71
'Three Sylvains,' 40, 41
Thurlow, Lord, 8
Togare's Bengal Tigers, 62
Tomkinson, 51
Tonelli, Miss, 109, 110
Toner, 51
Tournaires, 15
Trakehners, the, 27
Trinculo, 54
'Triple-in,' *56*
Trixie, 69; *99, 100, 101, 102, 103*
Trojan, 1
Trubka, Vojtek, 94, 96; *12, 124*

Ulrich, 51

Vail, R. W. G., 105
Velascos, the, 31
Vesses, the, 38, 42, 66; *66*
Victoria, Queen, 17, 21, 91, 106, 108, 113
Violante, 41

Walkmirs, the, 42; *71*
Wallendas, the, 38, 49, 50, 103, 109; *63, 64, 131*
Walpole, Horace, *quoted*, 9
Walter Guice Family, 109
Washington, George, 105, 106
Warren, Lavinia and Minnie, 106
Weedon, Herman, 110
Wesley, Roland, 103
West, 82
'Whimsical Walker,' 58, 59; *18, 77, 78*
Wild's Circus, 11
Wirths, the, 15
Wise, 51
Wolkens, 65
Wombwell, 21, 80, 81, 82, 83; *112*
Woodward, J., 103
Woolfords, 11, 15
World's Fair, 42
Wortleys, 38

Yelding Family, 15, 61, 62; *29, 80*

Zaro Agha, 62
Ziegler, Herman, 111

www.ingramcontent.com/pod-product-compliance
Lightning Source LLC
Chambersburg PA
CBHW051057230426
43667CB00013B/2338